Trumpets, Horns and Music

Trumpets, Horns and Music

by

J. MURRAY BARBOUR

MICHIGAN STATE UNIVERSITY PRESS

1964

To two lively granddaughters
JEAN *and* **KATHLEEN**
without whom this book might
have been completed sooner

Contents

Contents

Preface

The purpose of this book is to show how composers, limited to the scale of the harmonic series, evolved a characteristically high and melodic style for trumpets, the *clarino* style; how this style affected the general course of music; how the *clarino* technique was transferred to horns relatively intact, and was then modified in the early symphony; how the stopping technique for horns gradually led to greater emphasis upon a *cantabile* style, lyric and expressive.

This story of trumpets and horns begins a few years before Monteverdi's *Orfeo* of 1607. The heyday of the florid trumpet was reached before the middle of the eighteenth century and that of the similarly high horn only two or three decades later. By the death of Beethoven in 1827, the stopped-horn style had become firmly established. So the period covered is roughly from 1600 to 1830. The raw material consists of music with brass: operas and oratorios; symphonies and concertos.

If I were not an honest person, I might maintain that my interest in brass instruments dates from a conch shell in the attic of my boyhood home in Chambersburg, Pennsylvania, or from the mellophone which I played at Aurora, New York, in the late twenties. Perhaps it did; but the first real impetus to write this book came about twenty-five years ago, when Professor Otto Kinkeldey's seminar in musicology at Cornell University was studying Bach's *First Brandenburg Concerto*. I happened to notice that the horns reached the final cadence of one of the movements a bar ahead of the other instruments, with resulting clashes (see Example 79b). Curious as to the extent of the licenses permitted brass instruments at that time, I collected some striking specimens from Bach, Handel, and Steffani, and presented them in 1938 in the first part of a paper entitled, "The Use of Brass Instruments in Early Scores." Many of these clashes are shown in the fourth section of Chapter 2 of this book.

A year or so after this, I examined the brass parts in about fifty manuscript copies of early opera scores at the Library of Congress. The chief result was certain notational oddities that I discussed twenty years later in a paper, "Unusual Brass Notation in the 18th Century," which was printed with the same title in *Brass Quarterly*, June, 1959, and is incorporated as the first section of Chapter 1 of this book. (Caldara's high trumpet notes (see Examples 39, 160, 193) also turned up in this study. I regret that I have not looked at hundreds of other Baroque opera scores, for I am sure that there is further *clarino* brilliance scattered through them.) In the spring of 1946 I spent sabbatical leave from Michigan State University at the Library of Congress, where I turned my attention particularly to the association of brass instruments with voices, and delivered a paper, "Trumpet and Horn in the Church Music of Bach and His Contemporaries."

The stage was now set for my next sabbatical year, as Fulbright research professor at the University of Vienna, 1953-54. At the Library of the Gesellschaft der Musikfreunde and at the National Library, I concentrated upon brass parts in the early symphony. Franz Krommer emerged as an interesting writer of the Beethoven era, the result being a paper which became the article, "Franz Krommer and His Writing for Brass," published in the first issue of the *Brass Quarterly*, September, 1957. My thanks go to the editor, Miss Mary Rasmussen, for permission to print material originally published in the two articles in the *Quarterly*.

Strangely, Vienna does not contain a first-rate repository of eighteenth-century symphonic scores. I obtained permission to spend the last part of my Fulbright stay at the Thurn and Taxis Library at Regensburg, Germany, where in five weeks' time I had gone through the brass parts in 1650 works, mostly symphonies, but with a fair sprinkling of concertos and chamber works.

In recent years, as my long study drew to a close, I have made good use of the facilities of the Michigan State University Library, the University of Michigan Library, the New York Public Library, as well as the indispensable Library of Congress. Indeed, all four of these libraries supplied certain scores of Haydn's symphonies, unfortunately not yet available in a complete edition.

Let me express my sincere gratitude to the Michigan State University Research Fund. Two of its grants have helped greatly to defray the cost of the musical examples in this book.

Microfilms of horn concertos by Punto and Rosetti were kindly lent me by Mr. Nielsen S. Dalley of Lansing, Michigan, and I wish to thank him for them. I am very grateful to Dr. Birchard Coar for permission to quote musical examples by Cherubini, Dauprat, Gallay and Méhul, as presented in his book on horn virtuosi. Other individuals whose assistance I should like to acknowledge especially are Dr. Hedwig Kraus of the Gesellschaft der Musikfreunde, Dr. Carl Nemeth of the University of Vienna, and Mr. Hugo Angerer of the Thurn and Taxis Library.

My heartfelt gratitude goes to Dean Jan LaRue for the assistance that his monumental *Union Thematic Catalogue of 18th-Century Symphonies* has rendered in authenticating symphonies at Regensburg from which I have culled examples. I had been amazed by the scintillating horn parts there by a virtually unknown composer of Czech origin, Franz Xaver Pokorny. (Eighteen specimens of his style are shown in this book.) In a paper, "Pokorny's Extraordinary Horn Parts," at Ann Arbor in the fall of 1958, I discussed these parts and played twenty illustrations on the harpsichord. A few months later, at Boston, I played some of these passages again as a pendant to LaRue's paper, "A Musical Mystery at Regensburg," which has been incorporated in his "Major and Minor Mysteries of Identification in the 18th-Century Symphony."

The "mystery" lies in the fact that when the instrumental parts of many of Pokorny's symphonies had become separated from the scores, his name had been erased from the cover or a slip was pasted over it, with another composer's name substituted. When there was no original cover, a wrapper was made bearing the false name. LaRue located almost sixty symphonies with the double attribution, eight of which I had previously found to be identical, solely on the basis of the horn parts.

During the academic year, 1960-61, I was able to solve the mystery, thanks to a misplaced thematic catalog that proved to be an infallible lie-detector! By its aid I located more than forty new symphonies by Pokorny, in addition to the one hundred and nine already known. The villain who perpetrated the wholesale falsifying of approximately one hundred Pokorny symphonies was Baron Theodor von Schacht, general director of music at the Thurn and Taxis court and himself a gifted composer, although very much less prolific as a symphonist than Pokorny. A thorough discussion of Pokorny and Schacht will be found in my article, "Pokorny Vindicated," in the *Musical Quarterly* for January, 1963.

J. Murray Barbour
East Lansing, Michigan

Trumpets, Horns, and Music

CHAPTER I

Some General Considerations

i. Brass Notation

Trumpets were originally constructed in the key of C only, as scores by composers like Monteverdi and Lully attest. But, even in the prelude to his precedent-breaking opera, *Orfeo*, Monteverdi indicated that if muted trumpets were to be used, the pitch would rise and the other instruments would have to play a tone higher. At the time of Bach and Handel, trumpets were generally at the higher pitch—in D, the so-called church pitch to which organs were also addicted. Thus arose a problem of notation, which Bach solved by treating the trumpets the same as other transposing instruments, that is, by writing their parts in C. Handel, however, who very seldom wrote for trumpets in any key save D, always notated them at the concert pitch, with a signature of two sharps. (There are C trumpets in the *Occasional Oratorio* and in *Israel in Egypt*.) These two systems, the chamber pitch in C and the church pitch in D, underlie most of the anomalies in brass notation in the eighteenth century.

With the introduction of the horn into the orchestra in the early eighteenth century and with the gradual increase in the number of keys used for brass instruments, especially horns, it became the almost universal custom to notate both trumpets and horns in the treble clef and in the key of C. This was true of 95% of the symphonies, choral works, and operas which I have examined. It is the other 5% which concern us now.

Actually, in the middle of the eighteenth century, it did not make too much difference to the brass player how his part was notated. So long as he knew which crook to use, he could play the notes well enough, whatever the notated pitch, for they were confined to the harmonic series. But, at a time when the clarinets had not yet become an integral part of the orchestra, the only transposing instruments were the horns and/or trumpets. So it might make a difference to the conductor, if he did not have to transpose the brass parts in his scores.

A way was found by which neither the players nor the conductor had to worry about transposition of brass parts—the same method by which music students are sometimes taught transposition today. This was by clefs other than the treble clef, using the proper key signature. Then the conductor, presumably familiar with all varieties of clefs, would read the parts as written, without having to transpose. But if the clef had been rightly chosen, the players would read their parts in the treble clef minus signature, and would not have to transpose either.

This brass transposition by clefs bears some resemblance to the late sixteenth-century practice of shifted clefs in the writing of vocal music. If a clef was placed on a lower line than normal, such as a G clef on the first line (violin clef) or an F clef on the third line (baritone clef), some scholars today believe that the "high chiavette" signified that the music was to be transposed a third lower. Other scholars, however, think that the shift was simply to avoid leger lines, a long-established practice in the notation of plainsong. In any case, the "chiavette" notation died out almost a century and a half before the first known examples of brass notation with unusual clefs. (See the article "Chiavette. Chiave trasportata" in Apel's *Harvard Dictionary*.)

Table 1 shows how the transposition by clefs works. Eight different clefs were used, spanning two octaves, from the French violin clef to the ordinary bass clef. (The note following each clef is middle C.) The violin clef was suitable for trumpet parts in the keys of E and E flat, since it put the music a third lower than the normal G clef. Similarly, the soprano clef notates the music a third higher than the treble clef, and so was suitable for horns in the key of A, a third lower than C.

Although I did not succeed in finding examples of the violin and soprano clefs being used for E flat and A, the remaining five clefs were all used for transposing purposes for horns. (Each found use of a particular clef for a particular key is indicated by a check in Table 1, whether or not this represents a notational convention.) Example 1, from Traetta's opera, *Ippolito ed Aricia* (1759), is one of four instances in this one opera of the bass clef for horns in E flat. A sextet by Boccherini, Op. 42, an *Overture in*

TABLE 1. 18TH CENTURY "CONCERT" NOTATION FOR TRUMPETS AND HORNS

		Violin	Treble	Soprano	Mezzo	Alto	Tenor	Baritone	Bass
Trumpets	f	x (d)	x						
	eb, e	none (c)							
	d		x (d)						
	c		x (c)	x		x			x
Horns	Bb			x (D)					
	A			none (C)				x (D)	Trans.
	G		x	x (D)				x (C)	x
	F			x (C)					x (D)
	E					x (D)			x (C)
	Eb			Trans.		x (D)			x (C)
	D		x (D)			x (C)			x
	C		x (C)			x	x (D)		x
	BBb						x (C)		

G minor by Sammartini (T.&T. 6), and Lampugnani's opera, *L'amor contadino* (1766), afford further examples. The employment of the bass clef for horns in E or E flat is similar to the advice often given today to novices in score-reading: for transposed horn parts in these two keys, just visualize the bass clef and the correct signature, and this will effect the transposition, albeit an octave too low. Contrariwise, in Example 1 the bass clef and signature were given, which the players had to replace mentally by treble clef without signature.

The same opera by Lampugnani mentioned above is the source of Example 2, in which the tenor clef is used for horns in B flat *basso*. (Another instance is found in Galuppi's *Ifigenia in Tauride*, 1768.) This Lampugnani opera also uses the alto clef for horns in D, as do Leo's opera, *L'amore vuol sofferenza* (1739) and three symphonies in D by Charles Barbant Op. 6 (c. 1766). Unique examples of the mezzo-soprano clef for horns in F and of the baritone clef for horns in G were located by Kling in Grétry's opera, *Le Huron* (1768). (See H. Kling's "Le cor de

Ex. 1   Ex. 2

Horns in Eb (Concert Notation)   Horns in Bb basso (Concert Notation)

chasse," *Rivista musicale italiana*, Vol. 18, 1911, p. 122f.) For all of these combinations of keys and clefs, indicated by (C) in Table 1, the horn players would read in the treble clef without signature.

An interesting reversal of the chamber-tone transposition for brass occurs in the two symphonies by Navoigille (Op. 5) in the Thurn and Taxis Library. In his Symphony No. 3 in E flat the horns are transposed to C, but with soprano clef. If these notes are read with the treble clef and a three-flat signature, they are transposed back to E flat. This is similar to the use of the soprano clef for the "concert" notation of the key of A, for which I had been unable to find an example. However, a similar notation in Navoigille's Symphony No. 4 in A does find a parallel. Here the bass clef was used for the transposed horn parts, which, when read with treble clef and correct signature, transpose to A. The parallel occurs in our Example 1, where Traetta's "concert" horns in E flat, bass clef, would have been read in C, treble clef.

About 1830, which would be three-quarters of a century later than most of the examples shown of brass notation, Louis François Dauprat published a collection of horn trios, quartets, and sextets (*Partition des trios, quatuors et sextuors pour cors en différents tons*), to illustrate the color effect from combinations of horns with different crooks. Birchard Coar, in his well-known study of horn virtuosi in France (*A Critical Study of the Nineteenth Century Horn Virtuosi in France*, De Kalb, Illinois, 1952) has reproduced on Plate XV part of Dauprat's *Trio No. 6* for horns in G, E, and D, and on Plate XVI part of his *Sextuor No. 6* for first horns in C, G, and F and second horns in G, D, and C. The careful reader will observe that for each horn part in the

Trio, after the transposed signature, there is shown the concert signature of two sharps with the correct clef to effect the transposition: baritone clef for G horn, bass clef for E horn, alto clef for D horn. To these is added, in the *Sextuor,* the mezzo-soprano clef for horn in F. These clefs, of course, agree with those discussed here.

We now examine a different notational principle. Not only did Handel notate his ubiquitous trumpets in D at concert pitch, but so did many other composers. We can find countless examples of this practice in Italian operas by Galuppi, Traetta, and Jommelli, and some in Leo's *Dixit* and a symphony by Boroni (T.&T. 1). There seemed to be a tacit admission that the key of D was somehow different from other keys, that the players were so accustomed to church pitch that they did not think of this notation as a transposition.

The convention of the untransposed trumpet parts in D was often extended to horns also. But there were a couple of strange

Ex. 3

Trumpets in D (Concert Notation)

Horns in D

cases in which the trumpets were notated at concert pitch and the horns in C. Example 3 is taken from Pérez' *Mattutino de Morti.* Here both the horns and the trumpets are in D, the trumpets being notated in that key, but the horns a tone lower. (In the Crucifixus of Pérez' *Credo,* which is in E flat, this same notation is used, with the indication for the trumpet parts: "mezzo tono sopra.") This emphasizes the fact that the convention was primarily for trumpets. Jommelli made a distinction somewhat similarly: in four places in his opera *L'Artaserse* (1749) where both trumpets and horns play in the key of D, the notation is treble clef with two sharps; in the single aria with D horns in the accompaniment, the notation is treble clef transposed to C.

The church-tone notation gave rise to a whole set of combinations of keys and clefs, running parallel to those previously discussed and illustrated. (These church-tone notations are indi-

cated by (d) or (D) in Table 1.) The violin clef is suitable for
the key of F, as may be seen in Example 4, taken from the
Scherzo, the fourth movement of Telemann's *Violin Concerto in
F*. Here, with the trumpets notated with the violin clef, the parts
read as if in D with treble clef. In the passage quoted, the first

Ex. 4

Trumpets in F (Concert Notation)

trumpet reaches written d''' (concert g'''), the same top note
as in the *Second Brandenburg Concerto*.

At the opposite end of the compass, the bass clef is the church-
tone notation for horns in the key of F. There are many instances
of this notation, chiefly from the Italian opera composers men-

Ex. 5

Horns in F (Concert Notation)

tioned above. Example 5 is taken from Leo's *Dixit*. The fact that
the extreme keys are two octaves apart reminds me of a *Sonata
in F Minor* for bassoon and continuo, in Telemann's *Der getreue
Musikmeister*. The composer has stated that the melody might be
played also by recorder. This could have been done without
changing a note, since the violin clef, familiar to recorder players,
would automatically transpose the part two octaves higher.

More good specimens of church-tone notation in various keys
stem from Galuppi than from any other composer. In his opera
Alessandro nell' Indie (1755), he used the soprano clef for horns
in B flat *alto*. In his *Ifigenia in Tauride* the horns in G had church-
tone notation, which means mezzo-soprano clef. In the same
opera the alto clef was used for horns in E flat, and in his *La
calamita de' cori* (1752) the horns in E are also notated with alto
clef. In his *Alessandro* he even has used the tenor clef for the
key of C, giving an impression of church pitch! Finally, for the
key of A he used, in the *Ifigenia*, the baritone clef. In all of these
cases the horn parts would resemble the key of D.

Incidentally, Galuppi has made more errors in his use of clefs
than any other two composers. Half of the time the transposing

clefs were used correctly, but he also used the treble clef in place of the mezzo-soprano, baritone, and bass clefs, the soprano in place of the alto, and the alto in place of the tenor. Traetta used the treble in place of the alto and bass clefs, and Jommelli, on the other hand, the treble and the bass clefs when the alto was needed.

The most striking error in the use of clefs for church-tone notation occurs in Handel's *Jephthah*, the last of his oratorios (1751). The chorus, "When His loud voice in thunder spoke," is in the key of G, and the voices and all of the instruments save the horns have a signature of one sharp. There is a facsimile edition of Handel's rough score for *Jephthah*, and this shows clearly that the horn parts, which are notated a fifth high, in D, have a treble clef and a two-sharp signature, as shown in Example 6. This is exactly how the horns would be notated for

Ex. 6

Horns in G (Concert Notation is a 5th lower)

performance today, when the parts would be played on F horns. But, of course, Handel's parts were intended for horns in G—he has written in the margin, "C. 1 et 2 ex g." The correct notation, consistent with our other examples of church-tone simulation, would be the mezzo-soprano clef, with only one sharp. For this key Galuppi also incorrectly used the treble clef, as mentioned in the previous paragraph, but at least he did not tamper with the signature. It may be of interest that Handel has notated the G horns normally, that is, transposed to C, in both *Samson* and *Judas Maccabeus*.

It is wholly possible that the composers of some of the brass parts referred to above had no ulterior motive for using a certain clef, merely the practical motive of avoiding leger lines. For example, one of Mozart's early masses in C, K 139 (1771-72), has the principal trumpets notated with treble clef, but the unison *ripieno* trumpets with the alto clef. (In Jommelli's *Artaserse*, horns in C were given a unique notation with the alto clef.) In another early mass in C, K 167 (1773), Mozart wrote his *ripieno* trumpet parts in the bass clef, with the usual convention

of notating an octave too low. Again, when Rameau wrote for
D trumpets in his *Zoroastre* (1749), he used the violin clef for
no better reason, I suppose, than that he considered it suitable
for the trumpet tessitura. Similarly, when he wrote for unison
horns in G with treble clef untransposed, in *Les Fêtes de Polyhymnie* (1745), this stands out as a completely unique notation,
but it probably had no better *raison d'être* than to avoid the
transposition of a part. The same may be said of Traetta (*Ippolita
ed Aricia*) and Leo (*Dixit*), who used the bass clef for horns in
G. In his *Alarico*, Steffani has imitated trombone notational practice by using the treble, soprano, and alto clefs for his three
trumpets in C. These were all utilitarian usages, with no deeper
meanings, no esoteric implications.

One final usage remains to be discussed—"concert" trumpets in
the key of F, treble clef. Example 7, from Schütz's *Christmas*

Ex. 7

Trumpets in C

Oratorio (1664), is about a century earlier than the other compositions to which reference has been made. This apparently
unique notation, however, is not quite what it seems. Valveless
trumpets in the key of F could never have played the notes
here given, and besides we are plainly told in the score that the
trumpets are in C. And so there is no unusual notation; C trumpets can play the given passage and all of the other notes written
for them in this movement. The only puzzling thing is the B flat
in the signature, and that may have been added by the editor,
Arnold Schering.

To recapitulate: This eighteenth-century brass notation with
chamber- or church-tone suggestion, was rare, very rare indeed
if we except the key of D, and almost non-existent if the Italian
opera composers are omitted. The exasperating thing was that
all of the composers mentioned would use the normal C (transposed) notation for some movements and the hazardous clef-
notation for other movements in the same work. Add Galuppi's
addiction to wrong clefs, and the whole thing adds up at times
to a mess. Fortunately, the simplicity of the brass parts makes it
easy to discover the composers' real intentions by checking with

the other instrumental parts, even when the clefs did not correspond to the notes. Would that all notation problems could be solved as easily!

ii. Modulation

This study being concerned primarily with brass instruments that were limited in their scale to notes of the harmonic series, Table 2 shows the harmonics of a trumpet in C. A horn in C would sound an octave lower. Neither trumpet nor horn could play the fundamental, C, and only rarely was the second har-

TABLE 2. BRASS HARMONICS

monic, c, written. The natural seventh, bb′, could be obtained without difficulty, but was seldom used because its intonation was flat. The eleventh harmonic was much too sharp for f″, for which it most often did duty, and could easily serve upon occasion as f#″. Almost always the thirteenth harmonic represented a″, although it was flat enough to appear exceptionally as g#″. (See Chapter V for some of these exceptional uses.) Only diatonic partials were written above the sixteenth partial, c‴, an exception being Haydn's c#‴ in Example 123. The highest found partial for trumpet was g‴, the 24th, and for horn a‴, the 27th. (See the first part of Chapter IV.)

By their nature, brass instruments are more at home in a major than in a minor key. The bugle range, partials three through six (g c′ e′ g′) represents a major triad, and further notes of the tonic triad occur in the higher octave, c″ e″ g″ and c‴, partials eight, ten, twelve, and sixteen. The dominant triad is strongly represented with partials three, six, nine, twelve, and fifteen (g g′ d″ g″ b″). The subdominant triad is much weaker, only the fifth of the triad, c′ and c″, being present in the lower octave, to which the f″ adds an empty fourth and the a″ the desirable third; only in the highest range, partials eleven, thirteen and sixteen (f″ a″ c‴), is the subdominant triad possible in root position, and this combination of notes seldom occurs. The mediant triad is well taken care of, with g e′ g′ e″ g″ b″; and so is the submediant, with c′ e′ c″ e″ a″ c‴. The supertonic is least satisfactory of the major and minor triads in the key (the diminished triad on the leading note is no better), since none of its notes is available in the lower register—however, it might be represented by its seventh, c′ or c″, by the same license with which the timpano sounded C with the supertonic triad.

Thus within the major key itself the employment of the brass instruments brought about harmonic distinctions—the tonic-submediant and dominant-mediant areas having a superiority over the subdominant-supertonic area. These distinctions, of course, were much more apparent when the instruments were used primarily for their harmonic function rather than for pure melody, as with the lower trumpets when three or four trumpets were present. Once the confines of the tonic key were exceeded, the limitations of the brass became strikingly evident. In fact, there were compositions which hardly left the tonic and dominant keys while the brass was playing.

But the practice of certain composers is no true indication of the ability of the brass to play in foreign keys. First of all, let us examine the available notes in the primary triads of these keys. The seventh partial, bb′, had better be omitted, since it was too flat to be of much use; the fourteenth partial, bb″, should be included, since in this octave the player could control its pitch with his lip. The eleventh partial will serve as either f″ or f♯″. Although composers of the Bach era used certain other notes adjacent to those in the series, especially b′, none of them is included at present.

TABLE 3. INDEX FOR BRASS IN C

1	2	3	4	5	6	7	8	9	10	11	12	13	14	15	16	17	18	19	20	21	22	23	24
C	c	G	F	g	f	e	a	Eb	Bb	d	b	D	Ab	A	E	bb	g♯	c♯	B	Db	eb	Gb	f♯
37	30	29	28	28	28	28	23	22	21	18	18	17	16	15	14	14	12	12	11	9	9	9	8

Table 3, the index for the twenty-four major and minor keys, was formed in the following manner: any one of the four notes, g c′ e′ or g′, that appears in a triad is given a value of two; each of the ten partials from c″ through c‴, if found in a triad, is given a value of one; a partial present in the tonic triad is doubled in value; the index is the sum of the values of the tonic, dominant, and subdominant triads. (This amounts to giving the tonic and dominant notes of the key three points each, the mediant two points, and the other four notes of the scale one point each.) For example, take the key of e. Here, in the tonic triad, two points are given to g e' and g'; e" g" and b" one point, or a total of nine points. This number is to be doubled because it is the tonic triad, for an index of eighteen. In the dominant triad, B, the only notes present are f♯" and b", for an index of two. In the subdominant triad, a, two points each are given to c' and e', and one point to c" e" a" and c'", for an index of eight. Thus the index for the key of e is eighteen plus two plus eight or twenty-eight.

Admittedly, the index is not perfect. The relative minor key, especially, appears to have been given less than its due, for in Table 4, which reflects actual modulatory practice, all of the composers used this key far more than the mediant minor, although the latter occupies a somewhat higher place in the index. In the works of Bach and Handel, for example, there are many occasions when the dominant note, e' or e", is repeated or sustained in modulations to A minor. In E minor, on the other hand, no note of the dominant triad occurs in the lower octave except for the uncertain b', and in the higher octave the hazardous f♯", and, of course, an excellent b", which is a high partial almost unused.

If we were to lay somewhat more importance upon the presence of the dominant note of a particular key, the parallel minor keys, c and f, would rank even higher than they now do. Of these two keys, F minor was used by these composers very little, with or without brass. The far more common C minor included brass about half the time. But this fifty-fifty participation is very similar to that of G minor, a key in which the dominant is not available in the lower octave. And D minor, a popular key ill-favored by Nature for brass participation, had a higher ratio of brass use than either g or c. So composers did not follow too strictly a pattern of using brass in those keys where most notes were available.

The four parts of Table 4 which follow summarize modulations with and without brass in 107 works. After the name of the

TABLE 4. MODULATIONS WITH BRASS

(a) Handel

	a	G	e	F	d	D	b	Bb	g	A	c	Ab	f	Db	bb	F#
Concerto II	F	x	x	x	x	x	x	o	o	o	o	o	o	o	o	o
Dettingen Te Deum	D	o	x	o	o	o	o	o	o	o		o				
Israel in Egypt	C	o	x	o	o	o	x			o						
Ode for St. Cecilia's Day	D	x	x	o	x	o	o									
Samson	D	o	x	o	o	o	o									
Saul	C	o	x	o	x	o	o									
"	C	x	x	o	o	o										
Water Music	F	o	x		x	o										
"	D	o	x		o											
Total with Brass		2	8	1	2	8	3	2	2	3	2	2	o	o	o	o	o
without		5	1	7	6	2	1	o	3	o	o	2	1	1	1	1	1

(b) J. S. Bach

Cantata	Key	a	G	e	F	d	D	b	Bb	g	Eb	c	E	f
1	F	x	x	x	x	x								
" 11	D	x	x	o	x		o					o		
" 14	F	o			x	x			o	x		x		x
" 20	C	x	x		x	x				x				
" 21	C	x	x	x	x				x					
" 29	D	x	x	o	x	o				x				
" 31	C	x	x	o	x	x			x			x		
" 40	F	x	x		x	o			x	x				o
" 41	C	x	x		x	o			o	x				
" 43	C	x	x		x	o				x	x			
" 50	D	x	x		x	o								o
" 51	C	x	x		x				x				o	
" 52	F	x	x		x	x		o						
" 59	C	o	x	o	x	x	o							
" 63	C	o	o	x	x	x	o							
" "	C				o	o	o							
" 65	C	o	o		x	o	o			x				
" 66	D	o	x	o	x					x				
" 69	D	o	x	o	x	o			o	x				
" 70	C	x		x	x				x	x				x
" "	C	x	x		x					x				

Table 4—Continued

	Key													
" " 127	C	o	x	o	x	x		x	x				x	
" " 129	F	x	x	o	o	x	x		x					
" " 130	D	x	x	x	x	x								
" " 148	C	x	x	x	x	x				o				
" " 148	D	x	x	x	x	x								
Christmas Oratorio	D	x	o	x	o	o							x	
" "	D	o	o	o	x	x								
" "	F	x	x	x	x	x								
Magnificat	D	o	o	x	o	o								o
Mass in F	F		x	o	x	o				x	x	o	o	
Mass in B minor (b)	D	x	x	o	x	o				x	o		o	
" "	D	x	o	o	o	o				o				
" "	D	x	x	o	x	x				x				
Total with Brass		23	27	9	28	18	1	1	5	11	1	4	0	2
without		9	2	16	3	11	3	1	3	3	1	2	1	3

(c) Choral Composers

			a	G	e	F	d	D	b	Bb	g	f#	Eb	c	Ab	f	bb
C. P. E. Bach, *Auferstehung*	(c)	Eb	x	x	o	x										o	
" "Leite mich"	(a)	C	x	x	x				o					o	o		
J. C. Bach, *Passion Orat.*		F	x	x	x	x	o										
W. F. Bach, "Dies ist"		D	x	x	o	x	x										
*Gluck, *De Profundis*	(d)	D		x	o	x	x						o	x	o	x	o
Graun, *Te Deum*		D	x	x	o	x	x				x						
Graupner, "Ach Gott"		Eb	x	x	o	x	x				x						
" "Das Ende"		C,G,F	x	x	x	x	x	x			x						
Homilius, "Die Freude"		G	x	x		x	o			o	o						
" Passion		D		x		x	x				x		x	x		o	
Lully, *Te Deum*		C	o	o	o	x	o	o		o	o		o	o	o		
Marin, *Stabat Mater*	(Ab)	Eb	x	x	x	x	x				x						
Mayr, *Regina Coeli*		C	o	o	x	x	x										
Purcell, *Te Deum*		D	x	x	o	x	o	o	o	o	o			o			
Sammartini, *Magnificat*		Eb	x	x	o	x	x		o				o	o			
Telemann, "Der Tag"		D	x	x	x	x	x			x							
" "		D	x	x	x	x	o										
" "		D	o	o	o	o											
Zachow, "Lobe den Herrn"		A	o	x	o	o	x			o							
" "		A	o	x	o	x	x			o							
Total with Brass			12	16	2	13	7	1	0	1	7	0	1	3	0	1	0
without			5	2	11	2	5	1	3	6	4	1	2	4	2	2	1

*Gluck has no modulation to tonic key of horn, D major.

Table 4—Continued

(d) Symphonists

		a	G	e	F	d	D	b	B♭	g	A	f♯	E♭	c	E	c♯	A♭	f	g♯	D♭	b♭	G♭	e♭
Albrechtsberger	C	o	x	o	x	o	x	x	o		x			o									
"	D	x	x	x	x	o	o	x		o							x						
C. P. E. Bach	F	x	x	x	x	x	x		x	x	x			o	x		x						
"	D	x	x	x	x	o	o		o														
J. C. Bach	G	x	x		x	x			x														
"	D	x	x	x	x	o																	
W. F. Bach	D	x	x	o	x	x	x																
"	D	x	x		x	x	x																
Boccherini	C	x	x	o	o	o	o		o	x	o		o	o				f:o					
" (d)	F	x	x	x	x	x	x		x	x	x		o	o		x							
" (d)	F	x	x	x	x	x	x		x	x	x		o	x	x	x							
"	B♭	x	x	x	x	x	x		x	x	x			x	x								
"	D	x	x	x	x	x	x							o									
"	A	x	x	x	x	x	x		o	o	x			x			x						o
Danzi	B♭	x	x	o	o	x	x		x	o	o		o	x								o	
Dittersdorf	G	x	x	o	o	x	x		o	o			o	x							o		
"	F	x			x				x														
"	F	x	x	x	x	x	x		x	x													
"	A	x	x	x	x	x	x		o	o				x			x			o			
Eberl	E♭	x	x	o	x	x	o		o	o			o						o				
"	E♭	x	x	o	x	x	o		x				o										
"	G	x	o		o									o									

(a)

	Key																					
"	Eb	x	x	o		x	x	x	o		x	x			o						x		o
Fesca	D	x	x	x		x	x	x	o		o				o						x		x
Fux	C	x	o			x	x														o		
Gasmann	C	x	x	x		x	o	x			x	o			x			x			x		o
M. Haydn	C,G	x	x	x		x	x	o	x		o	x			o			x			x		o
"	C	x	x	x		x	x	o	x		o	x			o			x			x		x
"	Ab	x		o		x	o	x			x				o			o			o		
Krommer	C,F,D	x	x	x	o	x	x	x	x		x	x			o	o	x	o			x		o
"	F,C	x	x	x		x	x	x	o		o	o	o								x		o
"	Eb	x	x	x		x	x	x	o		o				o			x			x		o
Monn	D	x	x	x		x	x	x	x	o	o				o	o		o			x		x
"	D	x	x	x		x	x	x	o		o				o			o			x		o
"	D	x	x	x		x	x	o	x		o				o			x			x		o
Richter	F	x	x	x		x	x		x		x	o									x		o
Rigel	D	x	x	x		x	x		o		o										x		
Sammartini	C	x	o	o		x	x	o	x		o							x			x		o
J. Stamitz	G	x	x	x		x	x		o		o					o					x		o
"	D	x	o	o		x	x		x		o							x			x		o
"	D	x	x	x		x	x		o		x							x			x		o
Teyber	Bb	x	x	x		x	x		x		x	x	x		x	o	x	o			x		x
Vanhal	Eb	x	x	x		x	x		x		x	o	x		o	o	x	o			x		x
"	C	x	x	x		x	x		x		x		x		o			o			x		x
Total with Brass		33	42	8	26	21	8	1	3	9	3	2	2	12	3	1	3	4	1	0	0	1	0
without		1	0	19	6	14	4	6	7	13	2	7	9	2	0	2	3	4	2	1	0	1	2

composition or composer is shown the key (or keys) of the brass, the key of the composition, if different, being given in parenthesis. So, for Krommer the notation—(a) C, F, D—is to be interpreted as: this symphonic movement is in A minor, with brass in C, F, and D. The modulations have been calculated from the principal brass key, which for the just mentioned Krommer movement would be C.

In Table 4 it is easy enough to find works in which there is much modulation when the brass is silent and very little while it plays. For example, Lully's double-choir *Te Deum* in C is accompanied by trumpets and strings. It is in rondo style, with the trumpets used in occasional interludes only. The trumpets are used in one modulation to F; but in a, in G and e, in D and d, and in six other major and minor keys with flat signatures they are silent.

In Handel's *Ode for St. Cecilia's Day* there is an even more remarkable modulatory treatment, this time with only one trumpet. In the closing hymn, "As from the power of sacred lays," the trumpet in D is used in modulation to G and A, but it is unused in eleven other keys, and these latter keys embrace those which are the most remote possible from D—Eb, c8, and E. Or, take the opening chorus of the *Dettingen Te Deum*, in which three trumpets in D play also in A, but are silent in B minor and in four keys to the flat side of the tonal center.

In Handel's instrumental music, there are also examples of festive brass staying close to the home key. There is a $\frac{3}{2}$ movement in the latter part of the *Water Music* (the D major part) in which there is no modulation at all while the trumpets and horns are playing, whereas the Trio section without brass touches on two major and three minor keys. But none of the previous instances is as characteristic as a $\frac{3}{4}$ movement in the earlier (F major) part of the *Water Music*, where the horns play in C and Bb as well as in F, but are silent in the Trio, where the three nearly related minor keys, d, a, and g, occur. Somewhat later, in an Air, also in $\frac{3}{4}$, there is no modulation at the beginning and end, but the middle section, without horns, is in f and bb. The entry in Table 4 is a composite of the two movements in F.

If one begins to suspect that Handel deliberately chose to write for brass in major keys and to ignore it in minor keys, the suspicion can be confirmed by two other examples from his oratorios: in the opening chorus of *Saul* the two trumpets play in C, G, and F, but refrain from playing in a, e, and d; in the Aria of the Israelitish Woman in *Samson*, the single trumpet plays in D, A, and G, but not in b, f♯, and e—the Trio part of the aria.

Let us make a short summary of Handel's treatment of brass, based on the nine items given in the table: Although the supertonic minor key occurs in all of these pieces, the brass plays in this key only in *Concerto II*. The brass also plays in the relative minor in this same concerto and in the final chorus of *Saul*, but is silent in this key in five other movements. In seven of the nine examples there is modulation to the mediant minor, but the brass is used in none of these. Keys more remote than the nearly related six do not occur often enough to warrant any generalization except to say that the brass is not used in them—the sole exception being the supertonic major, which occurs in almost half of the examples and in which the trumpets do play in Moses' Song in *Israel in Egypt*.

With Bach the pattern of modulation with brass is quite different than with Handel. It is possible to find a few movements in which the brass is hardly used in modulations, as in the opening chorus of *Cantata 65* ("Sie werden aus Saba alle kommen"), where two non-modulating horns in C are used in a very animated obbligato at the beginning and the end, while in the middle the horns are silent as modulations are made to G, D, F, and a.

When Bach used four trumpets in *Cantata 63* ("Christen ätzet diesen Tag"), he approached the pomp of Lully and Handel. In the opening chorus the trumpets in C are used thematically in the introduction and interludes, modulating only to G; whereas the music without trumpets modulates to both F and G, and— significantly—to the three nearly related minor keys (a, e, and d), with a long section in e. But in the closing chorus of this cantata the trumpets are used in C, F, d, and e, but are unused in G, a, and D. Thus, even here, where Bach is greatly circumscribed by the large number of trumpets employed, the modulatory pattern with brass is determined in part by purely musical considerations.

It is possible to find in Bach also the careful contrast between trumpets in the major related keys and no trumpets in the minor related keys, as in the examples from Handel's *Samson, Saul,* and the *Water Music.* This is true throughout the *Magnificat,* where in none of the three brilliant choruses with brass do the three trumpets in D play in any keys save D, A, and G; whereas the relative minor, b, occurs without brass in every chorus; the mediant minor, f♯, in the first and second, and the supertonic minor, e, in the first and third, together with a modulation to C in the second and to E in the third.

In *Cantatas 66* ("Erfreut euch, ihr Herzen") and *69* ("Lobe den Herrn, meine Seele") the single trumpet in D and the three trumpets in D, respectively, follow the same major-minor pattern, with the additional key of b in No. 66 and g in No. 69. In the opening choruses of Parts 1 and 6 of the *Christmas Oratorio* the three trumpets play in only four of the six nearly related keys, although in Part 6 they play in the tonic minor, d, also. But in Part 4 of this work, the opening chorus is accompanied by two horns in F, which faithfully follow modulations to all six of the nearly related keys, while no different keys are used when the horns are silent.

Horns in F play in the same six keys in the opening chorus of Bach's *Cantata 1* ("Wie schön leuchtet der Morgenstern") and so do the three trumpets in *Cantata 129* ("Gelobet sei der Herr, mein Gott"). When Bach used a single trumpet he often found it possible to insert it in several of the less common keys, as in *Cantata 43* ("Gott fähret auf mit Jauchzen"), where in the bass aria the obbligato C trumpet plays in all of the keys touched upon —F, E♭, d, e, and g. Again, in *Cantata 20* ("O Ewigkeit, du Donnerwort"), the obbligato trumpet with the bass aria plays in C, F, G, a, d, g, c, and f—a total of eight keys! This is matched in *Cantata 70* where one C trumpet plays in a bass recitative in F, B♭, a, e, g, and f, and in a later bass aria in G, F, a, and g, or a total of eight keys. In the opening chorus of this cantata, the trumpet plays in three more keys, d, b, and c. Thus in this one cantata the trumpet plays in eleven of the thirteen written keys (omitting only D and E) employed by Bach collectively for modulations with brass!

It is clear, therefore, that Bach is far less limited than Handel in his treatment of the brass in modulatory passages. Naturally, both composers make extensive use of the brass in the tonic, dominant, and subdominant keys. But, whereas Handel, stressing the festive aspect of the brass, hardly uses it in the minor related keys, Bach finds these too to his liking, with the exception of the mediant minor. In the more remote keys, the pattern is different also, since Handel has only one use of the key of written D and none of Bb or any more distant key, whereas Bach, in modulations to keys with two or more sharps or flats, employs the brass three-fifths of the time.

Part (c) of Table 4 shows modulations with brass in choral works by composers who cover a rather wide chronological range, including Lully, Mayr, and Purcell from the seventeenth century, contemporaries of Bach such as Zachow and Telemann, and members of the following generation such as Gluck and the sons of Bach. So, actually, the median birthdate of this group of composers is not far from that of Bach and Handel. In Part (c) one quickly notices that the Lully *Te Deum* mentioned earlier is a very exceptional work, for none of the others has so great a range of modulation, or, more pertinently, makes so little use of the brass.

It is more difficult to find a pattern in the works of these choral composers than in the works of a single composer. One thing seems certain: these composers were not much concerned with showing a contrast between major and minor keys by including or excluding brass. In Zachow's *Lobe den Herrn* the two horns in A do not play in the relative minor key, both in the opening Sonata and in a tenor aria near the end. Mayr's *Regina Coeli* contains an interesting bass solo in C with two obbligato trumpets, in which there is an entire section in a and e without the trumpets—but they also fail to play in a modulation to the dominant key, G! Perhaps the movement that comes nearest to a major-minor pattern is the final chorus in D of Telemann's *Der Tag des Gerichts*, which has two trumpets and three horns, and in which the brass plays in D and A, and is silent in G, b, and f♯. But in the chorus just before this, a more normal pattern occurs in which four keys are used to one unused; while in the opening chorus the brass is used in five keys, including the relative minor, and unused only in the supertonic minor.

The brass was hardly ever used by the above composers in the mediant minor, both Graun (*Te Deum*) and W. F. Bach ("Dies ist der Tag"), for example, excluding it, although using the brass in five other keys, and Graupner ("Ach Gott") in six. In another cantata ("Das Ende kommt, der Tod"), Graupner uses the brass in all seven keys touched upon, but manages this by a curious variety of fundamental keys for the brass, with one trumpet in C, and one horn each in G and F, and timpani in G, A, C, and D. Note that in the single chorus in Homilius' *Passion* ("Nun ihr meine Augenlider") in which horns are used, they play in all five keys, the pattern running entirely to the flat side of the tonic. Note also how well C. P. E. Bach finds opportunities for his horns to play in minor keys in his cantata, "Leite mich," as well as in a bass aria in his oratorio, *Auferstehung und Himmelfahrt Jesu*. On the whole, the pattern for the choral composers comes much closer to that of Bach than of Handel, although Bach made greater use of the brass in flat keys—the written keys of Bb, g, c, and f.

Part (d) of Table 4 shows modulations with brass in the eighteenth-century symphony—Franz Krommer of the Mozart-Beethoven era is included and adds somewhat to the range of keys. These composers lived about a generation later than those in the first three parts of the table. Stopped notes were written for horns in some of the symphonies, and this increased greatly the possibilities of modulation. All of these symphonies were examined at Vienna, where I had more time for leisurely contemplation than at Regensburg.

So far as the nearly related keys are concerned, the pattern for the symphonists is much like that of the choral composers. The mediant minor remains a relatively unfavored key for modulations, and when it is used the brass plays only a third of the time. Modulations to the supertonic key occur less frequently than with Bach and more frequently than with the choral composers, but the proportion of brass use when this modulation does occur is constant at about 3:2. The overwhelming inclusion of brass in the relative minor key differentiates this group of composers most greatly from the others. Moreover, of the forty-four symphonies listed, only the first movement of Albrechtsberger's *Symphony in C* (1768) (DTOe XVI²[33]) retains the festive pattern for his horns and trumpets, as they play in the three major keys and do not play in the three minor keys. But even here there is a strange twist to the pattern, for the brass is used in a diminished seventh chord in B minor, the only time that brass is used with this key in any of the seven works listed in the table as modulating to B minor.

The symphonists differed markedly from the choral composers in the frequency of their modulations to extreme keys where the brass was usually excluded. Especially in the development sections did they delight in reaching out into regions rarely attained before. An outstanding instance is in the first movement of Bernhard Romberg's *Symphony in E flat* (not listed in Table 4), in which the development section includes five minor keys—g♯, c♯, e, g, and a (written f, b♭, c♯, e, and f♯)—in which the trumpets and horns do not play. Or take Duni's *Symphony in G* (also omitted from the list), in the first movement of which the horns have one seven-bar rest during which there are transitions to e, f♯, b, and A (written a, b, e, and D).

The above-mentioned movements by Romberg and Duni were not included in our list because they represented an unbalanced treatment of the brass. In contrast to them is the *Symphony in D* by Fesca. It is true that in the middle of the Finale of this symphony the brass is silent while the music modulates to G, C, E♭, e, f♯, g, and f. But e and g and even A♭ occur in the Adagio, with brass participation. The entry in Table 4 is a composite of these two movements, including a positive check for G♭ (concert A♭) and a negative check for e♭ (concert f).

In the first movement of a Boccherini *Symphony in A,* dated 1787 (it is available in a modern score edited by Geiringer), the two horns play in all four of the six nearly related keys which are used and also in F and a, but are silent in e, g, and c. That is, the written notes include a positive check for A♭ (concert F) and negative checks for b♭ and e♭ (concert g and c). Two other symphonies by Boccherini show the horns playing in every key to which modulations were made: in the second movement ("Imagine") of his *Sinfonia Funebre* in B♭, 1782, the two horns play in seven different keys; in the first and last movements collectively of his *Sinfonia Divina* in D minor, 1787 (the Finale is in D major), the four horns play in nine different keys.

We have already noted that in Graupner's cantata, "Das

Ende," the inclusion of the brass in every key touched upon was aided by his selection of three different fundamental keys for the trumpet and horns. But, although Krommer has horns in F and trumpets in C in the Rondo of his *First Symphony* in F, the brass plays in only five keys and is silent in ten, including B and eb (written Gb and bb). (This is one of the few instances among the symphonies where the modulatory pattern shows any connection with the festive aspect of the brass). In the Finale of Krommer's *Ninth Symphony* in C, however, the pattern is reversed. This movement in sonata-allegro form is in A minor until just before the end, with two horns in C (later in F), two horns in D (later in C), and two trumpets in C. Here the brass does not play when the key of Ab occurs in the development section; but there are nine other keys in which it does participate.

And so, although composers of the seventeenth and eighteenth centuries undoubtedly were hampered by the limited scale of the brass instruments, they made far greater use of the brass in relatively distant keys than is generally supposed. When, in choral works, they occasionally differentiated between major and minor tonalities by retaining or withholding the brass, this was usually done with deliberate intent, to preserve the image of the brass instruments, especially the trumpets, as symbols of festivity and pomp.

iii.　Crooks

The symphony composers, in particular, recognized that there were greater possibilities for using the brass instruments if they were not all crooked in the same key. Normally, the eighteenth-century symphony was in a major key, and was scored for two oboes, two horns, and strings. The woodwind pattern might vary somewhat, and there might also be two trumpets, and perhaps even one to three trombones. There might be trumpets without horns, but this was rare indeed. Not quite so rare was the use of four horns; but then the trumpets were hardly ever present, since the number of brass players was fixed, and the trumpeters were expected to play the third and fourth horn parts.

When there were four horns, they might all be in the key of

the composition, as in two of Schacht's *E flat Symphonies*
(T.&T.7,13) and one *Symphony in D* (T.&T.8), or in three of
Haydn's *D major Symphonies* (GA 13, 31, 72) and the Autumn
part of the *Seasons*. But, in order to obtain a greater variety of
open notes and a better blend, it was much more common to
have one pair of horns in the tonic key, and the other in some
other, nearly related key. When the composition was in a major
key, the key for the second pair of horns was usually the dominant, as in *Divertimenti in E flat* by Croes (T.&T.12), Klob
(T.&T.14), and Riepel (T.&T.19), all of which also have a
pair of trumpets in the tonic key, as does Krommer's *Fifth
Symphony* in the same key; or in the three overtures by Weber,
to *Freischütz, Euranthe,* and *Oberon,* in F, E flat, and D respectively.

Méhul's *Overture to Jeune Henri,* with its hunting strains,
even has six horns, four in the tonic key of D and two in A. A
variant of the tonic-dominant pattern is for the horns and trumpets to be in different keys, as in *Symphonies in C major* by
Joseph Fiala (T.&T.2) and Michael Haydn (DTOeXIV²[29]),
where trumpets are in C and horns in G, or in Krommer's
First Symphony, where the horns are in the tonic key of F,
the trumpets in C. A seventeenth-century use of brass in the
dominant key was in Schütz's *Historia,* where the trumpets in C
play imitatively in the opening Sinfonia in F. (See Example 7.)

Next to the dominant, the subdominant was the most favored
second key for brass. Thus a *Symphony in G* (T.&T.5) by
Pichl has horns in G and trumpets or horns in C, and the slow
movement in B flat of Beethoven's *Ninth Symphony* has horns
in B flat and E flat. The choice of the second key was determined
in part by the available crooks. Thus, in the first chorus of
Handel's *Giulio Cesare,* the key being A, there are two horns
in A and the second pair in the subdominant key of D; but in
the final chorus in G, the one pair is in G and the other pair in
D, which is now the dominant key. Franz Krommer enjoyed
these less regular combinations, having, for example, the horns
in the tonic key of A and the trumpets in the subdominant key
of D, in the slow movement of his *Second Symphony;* in the
last movement of his *Sixth Symphony,* the trumpets and one pair
of horns are in D and the other pair of horns is in G.

Since eighteenth-century trumpets were not crooked in B flat as often as the horns were, a composition in that key sometimes presented difficulties. A *Symphony in B flat* (T.&T.3) by Beecke has two horns in the tonic key and one trumpet in the mediant key of D, and the slow movement of Krommer's *First Symphony* has the horns in B flat, the trumpets in the supertonic key of C. In both of these movements the trumpets have their best chance to play when modulations are made to related minor keys.

Of all the commonly used major keys, A flat was the most troublesome, since neither horns nor trumpets were ordinarily crooked in this key. The almost invariable choice, then, for the brass was the dominant key of E flat, favored by both horns and trumpets. Ries's *Second Symphony* is in C minor, with the slow movement in A flat; the horns, being already in E flat, remain in that key. Ries's *Third Symphony* is in E flat, and so both horns and trumpets remain in E flat for the Larghetto quasi Andante in A flat.

Oddly enough, Krommer also has slow movements in A flat in symphonies which are in C minor and E flat, and his treatment of brass crooks resembles that of Ries. In his *Fourth Symphony*, one pair of horns and the pair of trumpets remain in C, and the other pair of horns remains in E flat; in his *Fifth Symphony*, one pair of horns remains in E flat, the second pair changes to the supertonic key of B flat, and the trumpets change to C, as in the *Fourth Symphony*.

An interesting example of brass treatment occurs in Marcel de Marin's *Stabat Mater*, in which the introduction, one middle movement, and the conclusion are in A flat, with the E-flat horns used each time. In the Andante con moto of his *Fifth Symphony*, Beethoven has evaded the issue of the brass playing in a movement in A flat; his horns and trumpets are in the mediant key of C for the express purpose of playing in the second theme, which is in that key. For completeness' sake—and perhaps to becloud the issue—it should be noted that the Adagietto affetuoso of a Michael Haydn *Symphony in E flat* (DTOe XIV²[29]) is in the key of A flat and the horns are directed to be crooked in the tonic key! In three of the four movements of a Vanhal *Symphony in A flat* (T.&T. 39) the horns are also in A flat.

Here are further anomalies of brass in major keys: in Weber's *Second Symphony* in F (1807) the horns are in the tonic key, the trumpets in the submediant key of D; similarly, in the Trio of the Scherzo of Krommer's *Fifth Symphony*, the four horns are in the tonic key of E flat and the trumpets in the submediant key of C. In the Overture to Rossini's *William Tell*, two horns are in the tonic key, G; the other pair of horns and a pair of trumpets are in E, the key of the well-known march. The submediant also occurs in a Michael Haydn *Symphony in C* (DTOe XIV²[29]), in the Andante of which the tonic key of G is not represented at all by the brass; but the trumpets are in C, one horn is in E and the other in D.

Beethoven's *Fidelio Overture* is in E. His horns are in E, but the trumpets are little used in the lowered submediant key of C. The trumpets might have come to life in a passage in C major, but there Beethoven has forced them to substitute for the timpani, a humiliating function also found in the *Choral Symphony*. The first *entr'acte* of *Egmont* is in A; the two horns are in that key, but the two trumpets are in the lowered mediant, C. The lowered seventh is not an uncommon brass key in minor movements, but what seems to be a unique example in a major movement occurs in the Terzetto in F in Mozart's *Idomoneo*, where two horns are in F and the other two in E flat.

In choral music, also, the tonic key is not always used by the brass, as in Rameau's motet, *Diligam te, Domine*, where the horns remain in B flat for the Ariette in E flat; or in C.P.E. Bach's *Auferstehung und Himmelfahrt Jesu*, which has a reverse treatment—the bass aria is in B flat, but the trumpets and horns are in E flat; or in a chorus in Spontini's *Vestals*, where the key is B flat, with one pair of horns in F, the other in E flat. Three keys are used by Christoph Graupner in his cantata, "Das Ende kommt, der Tod": there is one trumpet in the tonic key of C, and one horn each in G and F. By a careful selection of notes, Graupner has effective brass harmony.

It is in minor keys that the brass are most likely to be in more than one key—or at least not to be in the tonic key. In about half of the symphonies in minor keys, both the tonic and the relative major were used for the brass, as in Haydn's *Symphony No. 39* in G minor, with two horns in G, two in B flat. In the youthful *Symphony No. 25* in G minor, K 183, Mozart also has two horns in G and two in B flat. In the Menuetto of this symphony, the unison pairs of horns even supplement each other to double the melody played by oboes and strings. (Example 8) Kappey (*Military Music*, p. 53) has shown how a melody in G major could be shared by three trumpets, in G, D, and A. Con-

Ex. 8

sider also the extraordinary achievements of the Russian horn bands in which each instrument played only one note. (See the 4th Appendix, "Les orchestres de cors russes," of R. Aloys Mooser's *Annales de la Musique et des Musiciens en Russie au XVIIIme siècle*, Tome III, pp. 859-876.)

In the famous *G minor Symphony* of 1788, Mozart had only one horn in G and one in B flat, and so did Dittersdorf (T. & T. 23, Krebs 97) and Rosetti (DTB 29) in symphonies in this key. Similar treatment occurs in C minor: Haydn's horn in his *Symphony No. 34* in C minor are paired in C and E flat and so are Sperger's; Mozart in his *Mauerische Trauermusik* has two horns in E flat, one in C; the Funeral March of the *Eroica Symphony* has one horn in E flat, two in C.

Vanhal was fond of minor keys for symphonies: in *Symphonies in A minor* (T.&T.7) and *G minor* (T.&T.32) he has his horns conventionally paired in tonic and relative major. He included the dominant key in another *A minor Symphony* (T.&.T.6), with one horn each in A, C, and E, and also in a *D minor Symphony* (T.&.T.29), where there were two horns in D, another two in F, and a fifth horn in A. The latter symphony is dated, Regensburg, 1781. For some reason, the inclusion of brass in the dominant key for a movement in minor was extremely rare. Another example is found in Beethoven's overture,

The Ruins of Athens, where the key is G minor and the brass consists of two horns in G, two horns in D, and two trumpets in C. (Compare Graupner's brass pattern for the key of C major on p. 2.)

As with major keys, horns and trumpets may share two keys when the composition is in minor. In the Andante Allegretto of Krommer's *Third Symphony* the trumpets are in D and the horns in F, and so are they in a *D minor Symphony* Op. 1, No. 2, by Michael Haydn. In Zimmermann's *C minor Symphony* (T.&T.13), the first movement of Ries's *Second Symphony,* and the minuet of Krommer's *Ninth Symphony,* the trumpets are in C and the horns in E flat; while in the Andante of Eberl's *E flat Symphony,* Op. 33, the trumpets are in C and there is one horn each in C and E flat. Eberl still retained the E flat horn when the movement ended in C major. Krommer did the same thing in his *Fourth Symphony,* where the trumpets and one pair of horns are in C, the other pair of horns in E flat. Although the Finale is in C major, Krommer kept the horns in E flat, but, with the aid of stopped notes, they did not fare too badly.

When only one key was used for the brass in a minor movement, that key was more likely to be the tonic—at least in the examples studied. These are somewhat weighted by examples from choral music, as in movements in f and g in Pérez' *Mattutino de Morti* or in f and c in Marin's *Stabat Mater,* in all of which the horns are in the tonic key. (However, another movement in the Marin work is in D minor, with horns in F.) Curiously, in Bach's *Cantata 137* there is an aria in A minor with a *cantus firmus* trumpet in C. Among the symphonists, Karl Stamitz has tonic horns in e (DTBe1) and d (DTBd2) (trumpets also in the latter), and so has Haydn in symphonies in g, f, and d (Nos. 83, 49, 80). Asplmayr foolishly has both horns and trumpets in C in his *C minor Symphony.* (T.&T.2. He calls this a Sinfonia in Dis.) There is an Intrada from *Alceste* by Gluck, which is in D minor with horns in D, and he has one horn in D also in his *De Profundis* in D minor, where the three trombones supplement the four barren written notes of the horn, c', g', c'', d'' (concert d, a, d', e').

Some of the composers did prefer to have the horns in the relative major, as in *D minor Symphonies* by Huber (T.&T.6)

and Beecke (T.&T.1). Evidently the superiority of the tone of the F horn over that of the D horn for the intended function was the determining factor in this choice. Boccherini even had *four* horns in F in a *D minor Symphony* of 1787, and ran into some difficulty when the key changed to D major for the Finale!

The Finale of Krommer's *Ninth Symphony* in C is largely in A minor, with trumpets and horns in C, together with an optional pair of horns in D. Beethoven used a similar combination of horns in the Trauermusik of his music to *Leonore Proshaska*. For this music, which is an arrangement in B minor of his Marcia Funebre in A flat minor from his *Piano Sonata in A flat*, Opus 26, he had two horns in D and two in E. Similarly, in the first movement of Schubert's *Unfinished Symphony*, the key also being B minor, there are two horns in D, but the key of E is taken by the trumpets.

In the minor keys, as in the major keys, there are a few exceptions to general patterns. In the first and last movements of his *Farewell Symphony* (No. 45) in F sharp minor, Haydn has one horn in the relative key of A and the other on the seventh degree, E. (In the minuet of this symphony the horns are normal, in F sharp and A.) Beethoven, similarly, in the *Egmont Overture* in F minor and at the beginning of the second act of *Fidelio* has one pair of horns in F, the other in E flat. (There are two F trumpets in the *Egmont Overture* also.) And in the first movement of the *Ninth Symphony* in D minor he has one pair of horns in D, the other in the submediant, B flat.

Berlioz uses this same combination of horns as Beethoven (D and B flat) in his *Damnation of Faust;* but here the key is C minor, so that the keys of the horns are the supertonic and leading note. In the *G minor Overture* by Sammartini the horns are in the submediant key, E flat. Dauprat, with a battery of stopped notes at his command, used a horn on the subdominant (E) in his *Third Concerto in B minor.* Not so lucky was the very obscure composer, Joseph Bach (or Baach), who, in a *Symphony in G minor* (one of nine symphonies at the Gesellschaft der Musikfreunde), also put his horns in the subdominant major key, where they played written g', c'', d'', and f''. (Compare the horn in Gluck's *De Profundis.* LaRue has stated that this Joseph Bach was really J. G. Lang.)

Mention has been made of the difficulties which arose when the key of the composition changed from the minor to the tonic major, if some of the brass was still crooked in the relative major key. An *A minor Symphony* by Dittersdorf (DTOe XLIII²[81]), a Boccherini *Symphony in D minor* (1787), Krommer's *Fourth Symphony* in C minor, and an Andante in C minor in Eberl's *E flat Symphony* all showed this hazardous practice. But, in general, when the tonic major appeared toward the end of the Finale the horns would change from the relative to the tonic key. This occurred in the *D minor Symphonies* by Michael Haydn and Ignaz von Beecke mentioned above, with the horns changing from F to D; also in the Dittersdorf *G minor Symphony*, where the horn in B flat joined his companion in G, and in Ries's *Second Symphony* in C minor, where the change was from E flat to C.

A single change of crook within a movement might also occur when the horns in the dominant key were changed to the tonic, as in the Michael Haydn *C major Symphony* or in Méhul's *Overture to Jeune Henri*. A sophisticated change occurs in the Finale of Krommer's *Ninth Symphony*, which, as has already been mentioned, is in A minor, with horns and trumpets in C, and an optional pair of horns in D. Toward the end of the movement the key changes to C major, which suits the trumpets well. During the development section, the C horns are changed to F, and in the recapitulation the D horns change to C. A very different sort of change occurs in the Autumn section of Haydn's *Seasons*, where the key of the movement and of the horns changes from D to E flat, with the same sort of exciting (although by now completely passé) effect as a contemporary dance arrangement of a popular song.

Beethoven's *Missa Solemnis* is full of changes of crook for the brass. In the Credo the first pair of horns makes a change which is the same as the Haydn change just mentioned: at the Crucifixus they change from D to E flat. This same pair of horns is in *B basso* at the beginning of the Credo, than changes successively to D, F, and D. The key of the Sanctus is B minor, and Beethoven has put his second horn in E (the first horn is silent), the other pair of horns in D. The same keys are used for the horns in the Agnus Dei, but the trumpets are in what may seem the wholly incongruous key of B flat. However, the trumpets come to their own when the key of the movement later changes to B flat. At the end the key is D minor, and the first pair of horns joins the second pair in the tonic, D.

The crook may be changed in the middle of a symphony movement and then back to the original pitch later, as in two movements of Krommer's *Fourth Symphony*, where C horns change to E and back again, or in his *Fifth Symphony*, where C horns change to E flat and back. Everyone remembers the delightful effect of the statement of the principal motive of the first movement of the *Eroica Symphony*, near the beginning of the recapitulation. The first horn has been put in F for this little solo, and then returns to E flat. (See page 2.)

Usually composers allowed adequate time for the change of crook to be made, as in a *Symphony in D* by Klöffler (T.&T.3), where the horns are allowed eight bars to change to F and ten bars to change back to D. In the Amen section of Marin's *Stabat Mater* in A flat, the E-flat horns change to F after four bars' rest, and then back to E flat after twenty-two bars' rest. In the first movement of Karl Stamitz' *Sinfonia Concertante* in D minor (DTBd1), the horns are at first in D; after forty-three bars of silence, they play in F; after fifty-two silent bars, they again play in D.

The above changes were surely conservative enough! But in an *E minor Symphony* (DTBe1), also ascribed to Vanhal, Stamitz allowed his horns only two beats to change from E to G in an Allegro moderato movement, and three beats to make the reverse change. In the Menuetto the horns have only one beat to change from E to G for the Trio, in which they have a solo passage. In the *alla breve* Finale, the horns change from E to G with only a half-beat rest, then back to E with six beats' rest, to G with one and a half beats' rest, and again to E with three beats' rest. These are changes which are impossible to make, comparable to the strange notation which Wagner devised for his horns in *Lohengrin*. (Although I have read several explanations of Wagner's intentions, I am still completey confused. Fortunately, *Lohengrin* lies beyond the chronological limits of this book.)

The lightning change of crook indicated in the previous paragraph finds a parallel in the treatment of sordini. In the first movement of the *Symphony in G* by Michl, the indication "sordino" occurs twice, with only a quarter rest each time. In the Adagio of a Schacht *Symphony in B flat* (T.&T.14) the horns play "con sordino" and are allowed only an eighth rest to remove the mutes. In two *Sestetti in E flat* for horns and strings (T.&T.14,15), Zimmermann has marked the horns "con sordini" in both Adagios. But a later hand has added "senza sordini" in the middle of the latter movement, with no rest whatever, and then "con sordini" later with only two beats' rest. Again, in the Coda of his *Rondino in E flat*, a posthumous work, Beethoven has indicated echo effects for his pair of horns with "col sordino," with no rests. These examples all seem to indicate that the muted effect here was to be obtained by hand-stopping rather than by the insertion of a mute.

Table 5, which follows, lists the various combinations of crooks discussed in the third part of Chapter 1. If this chapter has helped to dispel some of the illusions concerning the restricted

TABLE 5. CROOKS USED FOR BRASS

(a) Major Keys

	Tonic	Super-tonic	Me-diant	Sub-dominant	Dominant	Sub-mediant	Leading Note
1.	X						
2.	X	X					
3.	X		X				
4.	X		x (lowered)				
5.	X			X			
6.	X				X		
7.	X					X	
8.	X					x (lowered)	
9.	X						x (lowered)
10.		X	X		X		
11.			X				
12.			X		X		
13.				X			
14.				X	X	X	
15.					X		

(b) Minor Keys

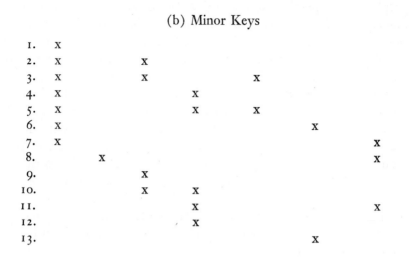

	A	B	C	D	E	F	G
1.	X						
2.	X		X				
3.	X		X		X		
4.	X			X			
5.	X			X	X		
6.	X					X	
7.	X						X
8.		X					X
9.			X				
10.			X	X			
11.				X			X
12.				X			
13.						X	

tonality of eighteenth-century horns and trumpets, it will have served its purpose. There *were* restrictions, to be sure; but even if a score in a minor key had only two horns, these were often crooked in both tonic and relative major, as we have seen, and so almost doubled their usefulness. And if ever-resourceful Bach in his *Cantata* 70 was able to give his trumpet in C something to play in eleven different keys, we need not feel too sorry for the composer who lived in the days before stopped notes and valves.

CHAPTER II

Clarino Style

&

i. Fanfares

The foundation of trumpet melody is the military signal or
fanfare—the bugle call, as it would be called in the United
States. It would be gratifying if the triadic trumpet figures in
musical compositions could be shown to be derived from specific
military signals contemporary with them. From the relatively
small amount of source material at hand, it would appear as if
the connection were not too close. Even at the beginning of the
seventeenth century the trumpet was assigned notes in art music
above the eighth harmonic, that is, in the part of its compass in
which diatonic melody is possible. So, if a composition contained
only triadic melody for trumpets, this was an artistic device,
an evocation of the concept of war or of civil pomp, either literal
or figurative. This being the case, there was no necessity to
make the imitation too exact.

Mersenne has shown, in his *Harmonie Universelle,* eleven of
the French military calls in use in the early seventeenth century.
(These are shown in facsimile in Chapman's translation of Mersenne's books on instruments, p. 334f.) For the most part these
calls do not rise above e′, the fifth harmonic. Valued more for their
rhythm than for their melody, some of the calls are monotonous
in the extreme, such as "A l'estendart," which contains twenty-
eight g and one c′, or "Cavalquet," which begins with twenty-
one c′, although it has more melodic variety later. The latter
part of "A cheval" (Example 9) contains the *sine qua non* of
trumpet rhythm, the galloping or dactylic motive of a quarter

and two eighths—more frequently, the motive consists of an eighth and two sixteenths. This call also has a dotted-note figure and ascends to the eighth harmonic, c″.

Ex. 9

Trumpet in C

Two calls given by Mersenne are for a trumpet in G, evidently pitched a fourth lower than the trumpet in C, for the upward compass extends to the tenth and twelfth harmonics, b′ and d″, respectively. However, since the former call ("Boute-selle") goes as low as the third harmonic, d, Mersenne has notated it an octave higher, to avoid the four leger lines for d. The second

Ex. 10 (a)

Trumpet in G (Concert Notation)

(b)

call ("Charge") for G trumpet is notated at concert pitch. (Portions of the G trumpet calls are shown as Examples 10 (a) and (b).) It might be added that even the eighteenth-century French calls given by Kastner offer little melodic inspiration to the composer, unless he is willing to abstract occasional fragments. (See Georges Kastner, *Manuel général de musique militaire*.)

Fantini's Italian trumpet calls of the early seventeenth century are, with a few exceptions, similarly barren of melodic interest. (See Girolamo Fantini, *Modo per imparare a sonare di tromba*.) His first call, "di Guerra," has a melodic curve such as we expect in a fanfare, and goes up to c″. Also, "la Rotta," although confined to a low range of partials, manages to ring a few changes on the simple motive of a descending fourth. (These calls are shown in Examples 11 (a) and (b).)

The early German calls are also far more rhythmic than melodic, and need not be cited. However, the little pieces ("Aufzüge") taken down by Hendrich Lübeck in 1598 are much superior to the calls contemporary with them, even if restricted to the same low part of the harmonic series. (Lübeck's pieces are given in Georg Schünemann's *Trompeterfanfaren, Sonaten und Feldstücke.*) The beginning of Lübeck's first Aufzug is

Ex. 11 (a)

Trumpet in C

(b)

Trumpet in C

shown in Example 12. Its march-like character is retained in a "Signal" quoted in a recent book by Speets (*De Trompet*). Here the repetition of the rhythmic motive of the first bar gives added interest to the well-planned fanfare melody, which retains its

Ex. 12

Trumpet in C

triadic nature even in a brief excursion to the higher octave. (Example 13 gives the first section of the Signal.) Speets does not date the piece more precisely than as belonging to the period of "trompetten en paukerkorps." Its relative sophistication would seem to place it no earlier than the middle of the seventeenth century.

Ex. 13

Trumpet in C

An interesting part of the manuscript trumpet music recorded by Hendrich Lübeck and Magnus Thomsen are the "Sonaten," which are variations on popular songs. In only a few of these do the variations show much resemblance to the present form of the tune, which is not surprising, since the eighth harmonic was the highest note used and it only seldom. The closest parallel is found in the third variation on the Christmas carol, "Joseph, lieber Joseph mein." The latter part of the variation seems to intone "Joseph" twice, and then varies the last two phrases. Examples 14 (a) and (b) give this third variation and my attempted reconstruction of the diatonic melody. (For another carol which might be intoning "Joseph," see Examples 61 and 63.)

A similar fanfare approximation of a melody needing a more

Ex. 14 (a)

Trumpet in C

(b)

complete scale is included with a group of coachhorn calls under the title "The Old English Air 'Buy a Broom.'" (Example 15) The tune is, of course, "Ach du lieber Augustin." (There is an undated American sheet-music edition of "Buy a Broom," "From Teutschland I come with my light wares all laden," which also

Ex. 15

Coachhorn

includes the original "Ach du lieber" tune and text.) Many of the coachhorn calls given in this little book are as lacking in melody as the early trumpet fanfares shown above. (The "little book" is called *The Coach-Horn: What to Blow How to Blow it.*) No. 5, "Slacken Pace," has some rhythmic variety while emphasizing the sixth, g-e'. (Like our bugle calls, these calls are all notated an octave too high.) No. 3, "Off Side," sounds like a jiggy version of "Slacken Pace." No. 7, "Change Horses," uses only partials two, three and four. (These three calls are shown as Examples 16 (a), (b), (c).)

Ex. 16 (a)
Coachhorn

(b)

(c)

The anonymous author ("An Old Guard") of *The Coach-Horn* describes and illustrates the difference between the coach-horn and the posthorn. The former is a straight horn made of silver. The posthorn has a smaller bore and is made of brass; for orchestral purposes it needs a tuning slide. The slide would have been needed in Mozart's *Serenade in D* (No. 9), K. 320, where a posthorn in A engages in charming discourse with a pair of oboes in the second Trio of the second Menuetto (Example 17). Its opening motive is strikingly similar to the coachhorn calls of Example 16.

Beethoven has introduced a posthorn in C as a solo instrument in the Coda of the 12th of his *Deutsche Tänze*. He has exploited the limitations of the instrument much more than Mozart has. The passage begins like the coachhorn's "Change Horses." Later, motives of from three to five notes are repeated several times in succession, as in the actual calls. At the very end, the coachhorn starts off much as at first, but with punctuating chords from the orchestra, and then finishes all alone. (Examples 18 (a), (b), (c))

For completeness' sake, reference should be made to an entire symphony in which a posthorn plays. This is a five-movement

Ex. 17

Symphony in C by Stephan Klob. In the first movement (Andante) the posthorn is largely restricted to tremolando figures in sixteenth notes; the most melodic fragment in the movement is shown. (Example 19 (a)) Of the other movements, only the fourth, Menuetto Allegretto, needs mention, for the posthorn

Ex. 18 (a)

(c)

comes to life in the Trio, the first section of which is shown. (Example 19 (b)) Here, like the trumpet in "Joseph, lieber Joseph mein" and the coachhorn in "Buy a Broom," the posthorn seems to be trying to express, half intelligibly, some diatonic melody.

Hardly any trumpet parts are specified in early seventeenth-century opera, save for the toccata introduction to Monteverdi's

Orfeo, and it is not pure fanfare melody. (See Example 29.) Agostino Steffani showed unusual skill at trumpet writing, some examples of his more florid style being given later. (Examples 31 and 32) The Allegro of the overture to his opera, *Niobe*, is scored for four trumpets and strings, and the trumpet parts, which are nothing but fanfares with imitation, clash audaciously

Ex. 19 (a)   (b)

Posthorn in C

with the harmony in the strings. (See Example 77.) In the introduction to the opening scene of his opera, *Alarico*, the three trumpets play fanfares, with canonic entrances, which are interrupted by cries of "Viva la Pace" from the soldiers and the assembled populace. (Example 20) In a similar festive mood, Bach, in the Finale of his cantata, *Der zufriedengestellte Aeolus*, bids his voices join the trumpets in a fanfarish "Vivat."

In the prologue to Rameau's opera, *Les fêtes de Polyhymnie*, the unison trumpets in D play a convincing military signal. (Example 21) Rameau has another seemingly authentic call in the ritornello of a chorus in *Zoroastre*, in which homophonic trumpets in E are answered by horns. Another excellent fanfare, for three treble instruments in close position, is to be found in Buxtehude's cantata, "Ihr lieben Christen." It seems perfect for trumpets in their favorite key of D. However, Buxtehude has scored the passage for three cornetti.

A very brilliant fanfare covering two octaves is played by the first trumpet in E flat in the introduction to the chorus, "Gott fähret auf," in C.P.E. Bach's *Auferstehung und Himmelfahrt Jesu*. (Example 22) Note the effective use of the galloping motive of an eighth and two sixteenths. His brother Friedemann calls his listeners to attention with a fanfare for unison trumpets and horns in E flat at the beginning of his *Concerto for Two Harpsichords*.

In a *Symphony in C*, Pichl has entrusted to octave trumpets

Ex. 20

and horns a forceful signal that ascends to c'''. (Example 23) This resembles somewhat a fanfare for trumpets and horns in the Menuetto of Mozart's *Serenade No. 3 in D*. The Haydn brothers also wrote octave fanfares for brass, Joseph in the Vivace of

Ex. 21

his *Symphony No. 97 in C* and Michael in the Presto of a *Symphony in D* (T.&T.6).

The most famous trumpet fanfare in orchestral literature is the call for offstage trumpet in B flat in Beethoven's overture, *Leonore No. 3*. (Example 24) Symbolizing the moment of deliverance for Florestan and the other political prisoners, it recurs

Ex. 22

note-for-note near the end of the opera. Less familiar, but fully as interesting, is the offstage call for trumpet in E flat in *Leonore No. 2.*

There are many other examples of fanfares in symphonies, but these are usually for horns alone. There is, however, one belated trumpet fanfare that is worth mentioning: in the Trio of the Menuetto of Krommer's *Ninth Symphony* there is a nine-bar

Ex. 23

Trumpets and Horns in C

fanfare solo for second trumpet in C. (Example 25) In Krommer's time the second horn had attained a tremendous importance; but this simple fanfare, occurring of all places in a minuet, represents the peak of virtuosity for a second trumpet!

Pure fanfares are naturally somewhat limited in number, except in situations where there is the direct association with an

Ex. 24

Trumpet in Bb

idea for which a fanfare is suited. Even then, the composer may not always restrict himself to triadic melody. A gem of trumpet melody is found in the opening movement, "le Reveil," of Morin's *La Chasse du Cerf*, which, however, is scored for horn or oboe. The beginning, with its repeated notes and galloping motive set in the higher octave, seems to be an authentic call,

Ex. 25

Trumpet in C

similar to our own Reveille; but the latter part includes passing notes in florid patterns of sixteenth notes. (Example 26) The whole is unmistakingly stamped as trumpet melody, despite Morin's scoring.

Another example of trumpet fanfares mixed with diatonic

melody is found in the introductory Sonata of Kuhnau's Easter cantata, "Wenn ihr fröhlich seid." Here the four trumpets in C, in imitative fashion, sound at first very much like the trumpets in Steffani's *Alarico* (Example 20); but later the smoother diatonic

Ex. 26

Horn or Oboe in C

style prevails. Example 27 shows the latter part of the move-ment (here reduced to two trumpets), which serves to illustrate both the imitative fanfares and the diatonic melody.

ii. Floridity

The florid melody in the last two examples is especially char-acteristic of a solo trumpet that appears in duet with a voice or other instrument. The concerted florid vocal style was of course an earmark of the seventeenth- and eighteenth-century Italian opera, examples of it being found as early as the duet between Apollo and Orfeo in Monteverdi's *Orfeo*. (Example 28) In the *Orfeo* also, in the famous Toccata for trumpets (an excerpt is given in Example 29), there is a hint of the sort of figures that would appear in the later obbligato trumpet parts.

Essential to the florid vocal solo are fioturas of sixteenths without leaps, already familiar to us from bravura arias in Handel oratorios. If a solo trumpet were to play either canonically or in thirds or sixths with the voice part, it would have to play the same little melodic figures. But the usual diatonic range of the trumpet in these passages was a sixth, between c'' and a'' only. (If up to c''' or higher, the possibilities were not so limited.) It required considerable ingenuity for the composer to make trum-

Ex. 27

pet melody interesting in such a small range, while fitting trumpet melody to the voice at the same time.

Of course, the trumpet melody was often varied by repeated notes and leaps, and by eighth notes or the familiar pattern of an eighth and two sixteenths—and sometimes these other melodic features dominated. However, there are enough examples of

Ex. 28

trumpet melody which abounds in groups of sixteenths, with an occasional dactyl or dotted rhythm, that one can generalize somewhat as to the sort of melodic motives that were found in a particular group of four sixteenths.

Ex. 29

Trumpet in C or D

An informal statistical study was made of representative florid trumpet parts in choral works by Bach, Handel, Kuhnau, Mayr, Steffani, Buxtehude, and Lully. (Some of the movements were for instruments only.) Perhaps only one characteristic section was included and repeated sections were always omitted. Even here there was danger, for certain figures were used overwhelmingly in a certain movement, and their total incidence would give a wrong idea of their place in the total picture. For example, the rhythmic figure of a dotted eighth and sixteenth was liked especially by Handel, and there is an aria in the *Occasional Oratorio* where the trumpet uses it exclusively—actually the figure here is a dotted sixteenth and thirty-second. Example 30

Ex. 30

Trumpet in D (Concert Notation)

Oboe

shows the trumpet in a homophonic duet in this aria. (In our analysis of this movement the dotted notes were checked as if they were all of the same length.)

With all the caution that must be exercised in observing the results, some very definite things emerged from this little study, as it is summarized in Table 6. In the first place, by far the most popular four-note figure was an ascending trill that would most

TABLE 6. FLORID TRUMPET FIGURES

often proceed to the next higher note, but might also fall a third
or even return to the initial note. This is (a) in Table 6—the
motion is significant, not the precise notes. Next in popularity
was the turn or concave arc (b), which would normally return
to the first note, but which might also descend by step or by
skip. (Both (a) and (b) occur in the diatonic portion of Example
27 from Kuhnau.) Other frequent patterns include a variant
of the concave arc (c), which also might have three resolutions—
up by step and down by skip or by step; the descending line
(d), with the following note a step below or above; the ascending
line (e), resolving a step higher or a step or skip lower; and the
changing-note figure (f), which would normally resolve upward
by step, but might descend by step. The inversion of (f) did
not occur in the trumpet parts analyzed, and, although the inver-
sions of the first three of the given figures did occur, they were
much less common, with the exception of (g), which is the
inversion of (c).

Of the eleven movements analyzed from choral works, four
emerged as conforming most closely to the norm for sixteenth-
note figures. Of two examples by Steffani, one is a very active
trumpet obbligato to an alto aria by Sigardo from the opera
Tassilone, 1709, an excerpt being shown in Example 31. The
florid D trumpet part in this aria includes figures (a), (b), (d),
and (e), as well as four less common figures.

The second Steffani example is a savage soprano aria by
Alarico, in the opera by the same name. The portion shown in

Ex. 31

Trumpet in D (Concert Notation)

Alto

Example 32 gives imitative treatment by three trumpets in C of a phrase that had just been sung by the soprano. The trumpet parts in this aria include figures (a), (b), (c), (e), and (g), as well as four other four-note figures.

Ex. 32

Trumpets in C

The most typical trumpet writing by Handel was in the chorus, "Sing unto God," in *Judas Maccabaeus*. There are three trumpet parts in D in this movement, a portion of the first trumpet part being given in Example 33. As in the first Steffani aria (Example 31), Handel's trumpet parts contain motives (a), (b), (d), and (e), as well as (g) and two other figures. In a part not shown in the example, the first trumpet reaches c'''.

Ex. 33

Trumpet in D
(Concert Notation)

Bach is represented by the instrumental introduction to the opening chorus of *Cantata 47*, "Herz und Mund und That und Leben." Here the solo trumpet is imitated in rather strict canon by the first violins and oboes in unison, the canonic interval being at first the octave and later the fifth and the third. (See Example 34.) So far as florid figures are concerned, this is probably the most representative of the four prime examples, since it contains all seven major figures, (a) through (g), plus one other figure. Here also the trumpet reaches c'''.

Not included in the statistical study is a chorus of Bach's *Cantata 31*, where there is passage in which the florid trumpet is imitated strictly at the upper fifth by the first violins. Like Bach, with the just-mentioned duets for violin and trumpet, Leopold

Mozart, in the Allegro moderato of his *Sinfonia di Camera* in D, has a duet between violin and horn. As Example 35 indicates, the style is largely imitative, and the horn ascends to written f'''.

In the other movements analyzed there is less variety in the trumpet motives, as in the opening Symphonie of Lully's *Te*

Ex. 34

Deum of 1677, scored for trumpets and five-part strings. Its melody consisting of rhythmically repeated notes and stepwise movement in eighths, there is a frequent occurrence of motives (c), (e), and (g), but no other motives were found.

Buxtehude's Easter cantata, "Heut triumphiret Gottes Sohn," is accompanied by two trumpets and strings. In its last movement, Alleluja, the principal motive is an unmistakable trumpet call, even when it is played by the violins or sung by the voices. The florid sections of the movement contain trumpet motive (a)

principally, although (g) also appears. Later in the movement, there is a dominant answer that takes the first trumpet up to d'''. (Examples 36 (a) and (b)) Not included among the eleven movements analyzed melodically in detail is another Buxtehude cantata, "Ihr lieben Christen." Its opening Sinfonia begins with the first violins playing a phrase that, both in melody and rhythm,

fits the trumpet, although the latter does not play it until several bars later.

The florid motive in the "Et resurrexit" of Biber's *Missa Sancti Henrici*, treated in canon by the five trumpets, includes only one of the common four-note figures, (e), the ascending scale fragment. (Example 37) When this is preceded or followed by a 3-1-2-3 pattern, such as e' c' d' e' (a figure almost unique in the works analyzed), the result is a happy play of three against four, relished by composers like Bach, Telemann, and Brahms, and very much at home in modern popular music—the classic American example is the *Twelfth Street Rag*.

Ex. 37

Trumpet in C

Duets between the trumpet and a solo voice, such as the Steffani aria illustrated in Example 31, are most remarkable, not so much for the floridity of the instrument as for the treatment of instrument and voice as equals. For example, there is a passage in the alto solo, "O sing praises," in Handel's wedding anthem, "Sing unto God," in which the trumpet, after preluding that includes figures (a), (b), (c), and (e), settles down to homophonic sixths and tenths.

Similarly, in Kuhnau's "Wenn ihr fröhlich seid," there is an alto aria in which, after an imitative entrance, the trumpet plays smoothly and homophonically with the voice. (Example 38) Here figures (a), (b) and (e) abound. (The opening motive is

Ex. 38

strikingly similar to Buxtehude's in Example 36.) In the passage shown, the alto strictly observes the brass melodic range also, so that the voice part could have been played on a horn in C *basso*. In the introductory Sonata to this cantata there is some imitative fanfaring after which the trumpets attain a more florid style in which motive (a) is prominent, with (b), (f), and (g) also present.

Occasionally there are operatic arias with trumpet obbligato. A simple example musically, but extraordinary in the range of the trumpet part, is found in a soprano aria in Caldara's *Iphigenia in Aulis*, in the florid sequences of which the trumpet plays almost wholly in sixths above the voice, getting up to e'''. (Example 39) Another very high note for trumpet (d''') occurs in an interlude of a tenor aria in the opera *L'Atenaide*, the first act of which is by Ziani. This interlude has sequences based on

the changing-note figure, (f), a figure which dominates the "Et expecto resurrectionem" of Bach's *B minor Mass*.

As a footnote to the discussion of the obbligato trumpet in an aria, the voice and instrument being usually on equal terms, mention should be made of the bass solo, "Since the race of time began," in Handel's *Joseph and His Brethren*. In it the voice and continuo parts are simple, the brilliance being centered entirely upon the trumpet, which ascends to concert d'''. Not all the florid arias stressed passages in sixteenths. In the bass aria, "Thou art the King of Glory," from the *Dettingen Te Deum*, Handel has only one beat of four sixteenths, but more than twenty beats of the dactylic motive, an eighth and two sixteenths.

Extended imitation between voice and trumpet was very rare, but there are a few choice examples. The bass aria, "Er ist's," in Bach's Ascension Day cantata, "Gott fähret auf mit Jauchzen" (*Cantata 43*), has an obbligato trumpet with an astoundingly high tessitura. Here there are some passages in sixteenths, but they do not predominate. The voice, trumpet, and continuo are treated virtually as a terzetto, as can be seen in the excerpt in Example 40. A similar terzetto occurs in Bach's solo cantata, "Jauchzet Gott in allen Landen."

The employment of a solo horn as an obbligato instrument with a solo voice was not nearly so common as the obbligato trumpet. A well-known instance of the rare association of

horn with voice is found in the bass aria, Quoniam, of Bach's
B minor Mass. Here the horn in D has indeed an important
melodic rôle, but it is not combined with the voice so intimately
as in the examples with trumpet. One of the more duet-like portions of the aria is shown in Example 41.

In Handel's *L'Allegro* there is a bass air with solo horn which
pays homage to the tradition of the hunt, but with only slight
suggestions of the French *sonneries*. (For a discussion of the
chasse see the last part of Chapter 4.) The text, "Mirth, admit
me of thy crew," is taken, of course, from Milton's poem. Toward the end of the air there is a captivating effect when the
horn keeps echoing the voice to the words, "through the high
wood echoing shrill." (Example 42) Benjamin Britten must
have known this effect when he set Tennyson's *Bugle Song* as
one section of his *Serenade*.

The first part of Example 42 has parallel sixths and tenths between horn and voice, as did Example 38 between trumpet and voice. Parallel sixths predominated in Example 39, and parallel tenths near the beginning of Example 31, as well as briefly in Example 41. Parallel thirds between brass instrument and voice are somewhat more hazardous, but there is a startling instance

Ex. 42

Horn in Eb

Bass

in the final chorus of Handel's opera, *Teseo*, in which the first trumpet and the sopranos have fifty-eight consecutive thirds. (Example 43) The second trumpet joins the other voices in rhythmic punctuation. The only text for this passage is the word "Goda."

Example 30 had shown parallel thirds between trumpet and oboe. Bach's *Second Brandenburg Concerto* is full of passages

in which the trumpet in F runs parallel to one of the other instruments of the concertino—flute, oboe, violin. In the first
movement there is a place where the trumpet and flute play in
exactly the same range, crossing as freely as if they were two of a

kind. (In Example 44 (a) the trumpet is notated at concert pitch,
for greater ease in following the two parts.) In the Finale the
trumpet gives out the fugue subject, which soars to written c'''
(concert f'''). (Example 44 (b)) When the oboe answers on the

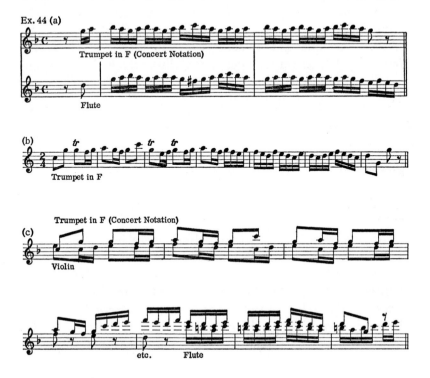

dominant, the trumpet plays the countersubject, leading to a succession of parallel sixths with the oboe a moment later. Parallel
sixths with the trumpet are also in evidence when the violin plays
the subject in the lower octave. But when the trumpet has the
dominant answer, the trumpet and violin are mostly in thirds; as
the passage continues, it is the flute that parallels the trumpet a
third lower. (Example 44 (c)) In the coda of the movement,
one will remember, the weary trumpet must again be able to
negotiate the beginning of the fugue subject.

Through the centuries, parallel thirds have been one of the
most common concomitants of the style when a pair of like
wind instruments is heard together. A prototype is the tiny
ritornello to the aria, "Nel puro ardor," in Peri's *Euridice* of
1600. This is scored for three flutes ("triflauto"), the lowest
serving largely as a tonic pedal and the other two moving in
thirds. Toward the middle of the seventeenth century parallel
thirds began to be written in profusion for a pair of trumpets,—
for example, in a couple of little sonatas by Fantini, 1638.
Schmelzer's concerto-like *Sonata Prima*, for two trumpets,
two violins, and four violas (1662), ends with sonorous harmony for the strings, while the trumpets play twenty-six parallel
thirds. (Example 45) Exactly contemporary with it is the
Sonata by Albrici for trumpets and violins, which also has trum-

Ex. 45

Trumpets in C

pet thirds. (See Schering's *Geschichte der Musik in Beispielen*, p.
278.)

Extended passages of parallel thirds were less common for
horns than for trumpets. In Handel's opera, *Il Parnasso in Festa*,
the horns in G were allotted forty-one consecutive thirds—very
monotonous, since the first horn played only three different
notes, e'', f'', and g''. In chamber music, where the horns were
likely to ascend into the highest *clarino* register, there were far
greater possibilities for horns to play in thirds and still make

interesting melody. See, for example, the latter part of a passage from the Finale (Andante ma non troppo Lento) of Touchemolin's *Partien in E flat* for thirteen wind and string instruments. (Example 46) The earlier part of this passage has a good differentiation between the style of first and second horn, but toward the end the parallel thirds are striking, with the first horn

Ex. 46

Horns in Eb

reaching e''' and the second horn c'''. Other illustrations of chamber-music thirds for horns occur in the Andante con Variazioni of a *Parthia in E flat* ascribed to Krommer (T.&T. 13/1), but probably not by him, and also in the Andante grazioso of a Rosetti *Parthia in F* (DTB 25[33]), which depends more upon stopped notes than upon high ones for its melodic interest.

Haydn's contribution to horn thirds comes in the Allegro of his *Sinfonie Concertante* in D (No. 72), which is almost a textbook illustration of the style. (Example 47) Here, as in Example 46, the horns reach e''' and c''' respectively. But there are four

Ex. 47

Horns in D

horns in this composition, and the lower horn is Corno III, accustomed to a *cor-alto* part. (There is an identical scale passage in thirds by Schacht in Example 60, again with the third horn playing the lower part.) Finally, let us observe a passage in that curiously archaic work by Beethoven, the *Sextet in E flat* for horns and strings. (Example 48) In the Allegro con brio movement there are half a dozen bars almost wholly in thirds. The passage is in the key of G, and, in addition to the stopped notes

Ex. 48

Horns in Eb

proper to that key, there are the chromatic lower neighbors, a#'', c#'', and d#''.

Although parallel thirds are an earmark of brass style at the middle of the eighteenth century, the brass instruments did engage in some polyphony among themselves. This was quite different from the canonic fanfares by Steffani shown in Examples 20 and 32. There is no difficulty in writing a canon in the unison if one never gets away from the tonic chord. But, in the polyphonic choral music of the eighteenth century for which the brass instruments supported the voices, it was usually very difficult, because of the limited scale, for one trumpet to state the subject of a fugue and another trumpet to answer it a fifth higher or a fourth lower.

Handel's teacher, Friedrich Wilhelm Zachow, contributed noteworthy instances of brass polyphony. (Handel himself rarely allowed his brass to become involved in self-contained polyphony.) In the opening chorus of Zachow's cantata, "Ich will mich mit dir verloben," there is a passage where the second trumpet plays the fugue subject, while the first trumpet is playing the countersubject. (Example 49) In a chorus of his cantata, "Es wird eine Rute," the two horns are independent voices in

Ex. 49

Trumpets in C

a fugue which contains twelve real parts! In still another cantata, "Dies ist der Tag," there is a similar treatment of the horns with the voices and other instruments.

In the opening Sonata of Bach's *Cantata 31* the trumpets in C play a canon at the upper fourth, in which the first trumpet reaches d''' and the second plays a couple of unorthodox c#''. (Example 50) In the following chorus there is a canonic duet at the upper fifth between the first trumpet and the first violins. (Cf. Example 34) As might be expected, the *B minor Mass* affords illustrations of polyphonic brass, the best exchanges between trumpets occurring in the fugue, "Gratias agimus," which also ends the Mass with the words, "Dona nobis pacem." There is a place in this movement where the first and second trumpets (the third trumpet part is omitted from our illustration) state the fugue subject in stretto, independently of the voices; the second trumpet continues with the subject, doubling the soprano,

Ex. 50

Trumpets in C

while the first trumpet doubles the alto part an octave higher. (Example 51) At the end of the movement the trumpets are treated similarly—the second doubles the tenor subject at the octave, and the first in stretto doubles the alto at the octave.

Ex. 51

Trumpets in D

The above type of doubling was very common in Handel's great choruses in D major, where the sopranos could be expected to reach a″ only at points of climax, whereas the first trumpet regularly went up to b″ and even to d‴ at a climax. So, in a very real sense, the brilliance of these choruses was conceived primarily in terms of the trumpets, with the voices providing the "orchestration."

Since the horns were lower-pitched instruments than the trumpets, the 18th-century composer was less concerned about their doubling of the voice parts. But there is a canonic passage in the opening chorus of Bach's *Die Wahl des Hercules* in which the first horn in F successively doubles the soprano in the

unison and the tenor and the alto in the octave; meanwhile, the
second horn is doubling the alto at the unison, and then the soprano in the unison and the tenor in the octave. (Example 52)
The first horn ascends to d''' here and also plays the unusual g#''.

In the period of the early symphony, with its extremely homo-

Ex. 52

Horns in F

phonic style, there are even fewer examples of brass instruments
being combined as independent voices. Richter, belonging to the
first generation of symphonists, seems quaintly archaic as he en-
livens the beginning of a short passage for two trumpets in a
D major Symphony (T.&T.5) by inserting alternately the typical dactylic motive. (Example 53) In another symphony in the

Ex. 53

Trumpets in D

same key he has expanded this motive to an ornamental resolution
which is mimicked by the trumpets in alternation. (See Example
93.)

The ever-surprising Pokorny has made the Finale of a *B flat
Symphony* (T.&T.82) a well-constructed fugue, in which the
second statement of the chorale-like subject is allotted to the
second horn, while the answer is played by the first horn in a
tessitura that brings him to e'''. (Here the high tessitura is an indication that the horns are in *B basso*.) When the first horn is
given the subject later in the movement, the second horn has a
counter melody. (Examples 54 (a) and (b)) This is one of five
Pokorny symphonies which appear under the name of Besch.

If Pokorny's fugue seems to belong to a previous era, what
shall we say of the fugal writing with brass in the Finale of the
Choral Symphony? In the Allegro energico section the brass pro-
vide a curious reënforcement of the fugue subject and answer:

the altos are supported by unison clarinets, second violins, and the first trombone, together with the unison trumpets in D so far as their scale enables them to play. The omitted notes (f', a', b') are shown in brackets in Example 55. Immediately after this, the unison horns in D and other instruments similarly support the tenors—note the tonal answer. The horns play b', but omit the easy f#'', which corresponds to the trumpet's omitted b'.

But such strict polyphonic treatment of the brass as Pokorny and Beethoven have shown was almost non-existent in the symphonic era. Canonic imitation, if present at all, might be like the jolly little fanfare in the Menuetto of a Dittersdorf *D major Symphony* (T.&T.23)—the composer has proudly labeled the

passage "canone." (Example 56) Or it might be like the canon between unison trumpets and octave horns in the coda of the Finale of Krommer's *Second Symphony* in D. This fanfare motive (part of the second subject) had been presented homophonically by the brass in the exposition and recapitulation, and is all

the more effective for its staggered presentation at the end of the movement. (Example 57)

Imitative writing for horns, or at least a considerable degree of melodic independence, might be looked for in a double concerto, where the composer would expect the players to have the

Ex. 57

Trumpets in D

Horns in D

technique necessary to negotiate the notes of the *clarino* register. This is splendidly illustrated in a Pokorny *Concerto da Camera in E flat* for horns and strings, dated Hohenaltheim, September 14, 1754. (T.&T.158) In the passage quoted in Example 58, the first horn goes so high (f''') that the second horn can imitate it at the lower seventh without resorting to stopped notes. Of

Ex. 58

Horns in Eb

course, the date of this work was earlier than Hampel's invention of stopping, so that the g#'', not uncommon in Pokorny's horn writing, must have been played as the 13th partial. There is another g#'', for example, in the Pokorny *Concerto for Two Horns in F*, in a passage in which the first horn smoothly imitates a figure in triplet sixteenths initiated by the second horn. (Example 59) (The parts for this concerto, at the Thurn and Taxis Library, had been provisionally assigned to Sterkel.)

Our final example of horn polyphony is by Pokorny's colleague at Regensburg, Theodor von Schacht. It is from a *Symphony in D* (T.&T.8), dated Regensburg, 1779. This symphony was for a large orchestra, including oboes, clarinets, flutes, four horns, trumpets and timpani, and strings, with "cembalo ob-

bligato." According to the parts, the horns were played by
Rudolf, Fritsch, Weiss, and Stumm. Example 60 shows the four
horns at their brilliant best, in a passage which is responsorial
without being strictly imitative. Triplet sixteenths are again very
much in evidence. The first and third horns go scalewise to e'''

and c''' respectively, precisely as in Haydn's *Sinfonie Concertante*. (Example 47) Note that this same scale in thirds, which
began Example 46, was there written by another Regensburg
composer, Touchemolin.

In conclusion, let us remind ourselves again that the high, florid
type of brass writing in the eighteenth century was associated
chiefly with the trumpet, as the common name (*clarino*) for the

tessitura and the style indicates. It was the trumpet rather than
the horn that, in the late Baroque operas and oratorios, was
usually called upon to blend smoothly with the human voice and
to follow the voice most adeptly in all of its divagations. In the

oratorios, too, where the polyphonic style prevailed, trumpets were more likely than horns to be involved in the polyphony. (The next section of this book shows what happened when the brass were associated with voices in music of a more homophonic type.) Except for the eventual lowering of the tessitura, more than balanced by the addition of stopped notes, the horns in the Classical symphony were as well suited to playing in counterpoint as were the trumpets of the previous generations. But, by and large, the *early* symphony had little use for counterpoint. And so we hail the music of the Regensburg masters—Pokorny, Schacht, Touchemolin—as a glittering exception, and its composers as an exclusive fraternity, to which we admit, as honorary members, Bach (Example 52), Haydn (Example 47), and Beethoven (Example 48).

iii.   Brass with the Chorale

When the composer of choral music was writing a festive chorus with trumpets, he was free to pattern his vocal motives upon trumpet idiom, as we have already seen. Under proper handling, the trumpets and/or the horns might even engage in polyphonic discourse among themselves, as has just been discussed. But when the brass was used with a predetermined melody, such as a chorale, the composer was confronted with a different sort of problem. The entire chorale melody could be played by the brass instrument, if it were "authentic," that is, if it lay between the keynote and its octave. A melody like "My country 'tis of thee" or the "plagal" "Come, Thou almighty King" would have presented no problem either; the leading note found in both melodies had long been in use, and the only other note in either which is below the tonic is the dominant in the latter melody.

But, even if the melody were playable on the first horn or trumpet, there remained the troublesome question of finding suitable notes in the arpeggio part of its compass for the second horn or trumpet to play. Since the harmony of a chorale was to a large extent predetermined also, the choice was difficult to make. A typical chorale melody in the authentic mode is "Wie

schön leuchtet der Morgenstern." In the key of F, its compass is
from f' to f"; it is entirely diatonic and presents no real problems.

Example 61 shows Kuhnau's setting of the above chorale, in
his cantata of the same name. We show the horn and voice parts

only; where there are rests, the strings are playing. There is nothing really wrong with the second horn part, except for a lack of
imagination. To our ears the horn fourth in every cadence save
the final one gives a very bare effect. On the other hand, there
are effective horn fourths on the first syllable of the spondee
words "lieblich, freundlich," just following the repetition of the
first three phrases, for here they seem like appoggiaturas.

It will not be a digression to remind the reader (see p. 9)
that brass fourths were almost inescapable when the subdominant
triad occurred. Bach bowed to the inevitable in an illustration
later in this section. (Example 64) Beethoven marred a fine hunting tune in the Vivace of his *Seventh Symphony* by two prominent horn fourths with subdominant harmony, and wrote an
almost dissonant eleventh in the Allegretto (the Shepherds' Song)
of the *Sixth Symphony*. In the final chorus of *Esther*, "The Lord
our enemy has slain," there is a modulation to the subdominant
key, in which Handel has his trumpets play concert d' d" g"
four times, with the kettledrum also playing a D each time.
(Example 62)

Ex. 62

Trumpets in D (Concert Notation)

But in Example 61 none of the horn fourths occurs with subdominant harmony. (The subdominant occurs in the third phrase
and again in the last phrase; both times the horns play f" a".)
They occur when the melody note is either the dominant or
the tonic, and the horns might have been in octaves rather than
in fourths. Kuhnau just wrote the fourths because he liked them.
They were definitely an earmark of the older brass style that
was to become archaic a generation or two later. So Bach's
"Gratias" (Example 51) flaunts two superfluous cadential
fourths. Handel, too, was fond of the fourths, writing them, for
example, in dominant cadences of his "See, the conquering hero
comes," from *Judas Maccabaeus*. (This is a later part than Example 109.) Sometimes, one might add, a tonic or dominant
fourth for trumpets was supported by the kettledrum, but this
practice did not help the empty fourths for horns. (In bars one

and three of Example 62 there is drum support for a tonic $\frac{6}{4}$.)

It is interesting to compare Kuhnau's treatment of this Advent chorale, "Wie schön," with Bach's, as found in his *Cantata 1*. (Example 63) His harmony is slightly different from Kuhnau's, but that is unimportant. The striking thing is that, with the

melody also being played by the first horn throughout, Bach has given the second horn a most interesting and florid part, which adds real distinction to his setting. In the cadence at the sixth bar the e' (concert a) in the second horn clashes with the dominant harmony, even though there is a 4-3 suspension to explain the c'. The justification is that the tenor is singing the same note, a, as a passing note between g and b♭, and so the clash must be considered a parasitic dissonance rather than a common brass cadential license. (Compare the final section of this chapter.) Bach has a similar parasitic dissonance with horns in the homophonic chorale setting in *Cantata 128*.

Kuhnau and Bach were lucky in their melody and harmony. A more normal situation arises in the melody for "Gelobet seist du, Jesu Christ," for in the third phrase it descends stepwise to the dominant, including the concert e' (written a'), unplayable on a G horn. (For Bach's treatment of similar plagal tunes see Examples 68 and 70.) There is an implied modulation to the subdominant key in the first phrase, and the subdominant occurs as well in the plagal cadence of the final phrase. Let us observe how Bach has surmounted these hurdles in his *Cantata 91*. (Example 64) On the first beat of the first bar there is subdominant harmony in the parts not shown here; Bach has given the second horn the octave, c', for this beat. On the first and third beats

of the second bar, where the written melody note is the subdominant root, f'', there is nothing better for the second horn
than the weak fourth, c''. Note that in the sixth bar there is
the fourth, d'' (unnecessarily), below the dominant, g''. It is in
this bar that the chorale melody falls by step to the dominant, and

Ex. 64

Bach has kept out of trouble by not doubling the melody here,
but having both horns above the melody. In the final bar, as
the melody ends with a chant-like "Kyrie eleison," there was po-
tential danger also, for there was the plagal cadence to consider.
He has solved this last problem in a characteristically brilliant
way by giving his horns a florid ending that takes the first horn
up to his c''' (concert g'').

There is another way to get around the difficulty of the plagal
melody that descends by step: put the horns in a key which is a
fifth lower than that of the chorale melody, and then the entire
melody will lie in the horn's diatonic range. In the chorale just
discussed, "Gelobet seist du," this would mean putting the horns
in C, with e''' the top note for first horn. There are two things
wrong with this idea: Bach seldom wrote for horns in C, and
apparently he never wrote a note higher than d''' for either
trumpet or horn. But we have already noted that e''' *was* written
in the eighteenth century (Examples 46, 47, 60) and even f'''
(Example 58). So Example 65 shows how Bach might have
written for second horn if he had been using horns in C in
Cantata 91. Except for the first and last phrases and the cadence

at bar six, I have retained most of Bach's own partwriting; in the final cadence, I have preserved an ornamental flourish.

In a minor key there might have been little opportunity for the first horn to play the melody and even less for the second horn to play a respectable melodic line. And yet a resourceful

Ex. 65

Horns in C

composer took advantage of such opportunities as were present. For example, in Bach's *Cantata 14*, "Wär' Gott nicht mit uns diese Zeit," the soprano melody, in the closing chorale in G minor, is supported by the corno di caccia, two oboes, and the first violins. Although the horn part is not given separately, presumably the horn is in F, since that was the key of the first movement of the cantata, with the horn playing. In the course of the melody b' occurs as an accidental five times. That would be easy for the horn in F, for the note would be the written f#', the eleventh harmonic. (Example 66)

Ex. 66

(Possible for Horn in F)

Charles Sanford Terry, in his book, *Bach's Orchestra*, has included the above movement among some ninety movements in forty-seven cantatas, for which he was certain the Zugtrompete, or *tromba (Corno) da tirarsi*, must have been used. This was the mysterious trumpet with the single slide, which many authorities believe never did exist, the name being Bach's way of designating the soprano trombone. Bach himself has prescribed the *tromba da tirarsi* in only six cantatas, for a total of thirteen movements. But it is certainly true that in many other movements where Bach has simply indicated that the "Tromba" or "Corno" was to play in unison with the sopranos on the chorale melody, this would have been impossible on any ordinary trumpet or horn.

In listing seven times as many movements as the composer himself has indicated, however, Terry has gone much too far. I have examined the scale for all the movements listed by Terry and found that half of them could be played on the natural horn: eleven each on the F horn and the D horn, eight on the C horn, seven on the G horn, four on the Eb horn, and two each on the A horn and Bb *basso* horn. Some of the remaining movements contain a part that moves rather rapidly and in a style alien to brass instruments. They would seem to have been intended for the *cornetto*, which Bach has indicated by name in only eleven cantatas. It is interesting to observe that Handel has written an obbligato *tromba* part to the tenor aria in A minor, "With honor let desert be crowned," in *Judas Maccabaeus*. The entire style and scale of this obbligato part suggest the *cornetto*.

Terry has also made a couple of amusing slips in the opposite direction: In *Cantata 110* there is a very short diatonic scale— b', c#", d", e", f#". For this cantata Terry has prescribed the ordinary trumpet. But this sequence of notes would not be possible except on an A trumpet, which Bach apparently never used. For a chorus in *Cantata 77* Terry has also listed the ordinary trumpet. But the scale commences g', bb', c", and continues with every semitone in the next octave! This would have been impossible on an eighteenth-century trumpet at any pitch. The question of the *tromba da tirarsi* is somewhat alien to the main current of discussion in this book. But I would like to assert that, on this matter at least, Terry is completely undependable.

Let us return now to the problems involved with using brass in a minor key. Sebastian's son, Emmanuel, was a master at the art of writing for horns in a minor key. In his cantata, "Leite mich," the horns in C play with the first stanza of the A-minor chorale, and again with the third stanza, with different harmonization. Both settings have many interesting features; Example 67 gives the parts for horns and voices in the second setting. There are hardly any rests for the horns, despite the chromaticism and borrowed chords. The horns are able to play with chromatic and diminished sevenths, and, in the first setting, with a diminished triad and an augmented sixth. Emmanuel has made

Ex. 67

Horns in C

Voices

no special effort to have the horns play the melody (the attempt would have been futile, anyway), but they add greatly to the rich harmonic texture.

When three valveless brass instruments played with a chorale, the composer had an acute problem of finding notes for his

players if the harmony was much more complicated than tonic
and dominant chords. We saw in Example 62 how Handel was
handicapped in a simple modulation to the subdominant key.
And yet for all festive occasions three trumpets were *de rigueur*.
Bach, in his *Cantata 130*, "Herr Gott, dich loben alle wir," had
to cope with the further difficulty that the chorale melody lies

Ex. 68

in the plagal range. It is our familiar *Old Hundredth*, here in
triple meter. Bach has neatly avoided the complicated issue by
introducing his soaring trumpets as obbligato instruments in the
second half of each phrase. Example 68 shows how the first
phrase is treated. As with the chorale in Example 64, it is quite
possible for the *Old Hundredth* melody to be played by horns
in F, provided they play in the written key of G. Here the high
note is d″. (Example 69)

Ex. 69

Another solution for the problem of having the brass play with
a plagal melody is to ignore the chorale line completely, and to
have the instruments play in their highest tessitura. This is what
Bach has done in *Cantata 137*, "Lobe den Herren." With the

three trumpets and four voices, there are seven real parts, which makes for some angularity in the tenor line. (Example 70) It is to be hoped that both here and in Example 68 the oboes, strings, and (especially) the organ gave sufficient support to the voices that the trumpet tone did not predominate.

Ex. 70

Trumpets in C

Voices

The *Passion Chorale* ("O Sacred Head") is an authentic melody which is difficult for brass only because it extends in the seventh phrase to the 18th partial, d'''. However, all of the high notes are approached gradually, and the construction of the tune makes it simple to drop the brass, if desired, in the fifth and sixth phrases, for contrast and their relief. But Bach, in his festive setting of this melody in the *Christmas Oratorio*, does not assign it to the first trumpet at all. The trumpet is given instead a florid melodic line of authentic Bach vintage, which, with full co-öperation on the part of the oboes and strings, forms the basis of the prelude, postlude, and interludes. The second and third trumpets are kept discreetly in the background. The twelve-bar

Ex. 71

Trumpet in D

prelude returns complete after the second phrase; after the fourth phrase its first four bars are heard; then—a typical Bach touch!—as the following four bars are played as the third interlude, the voices enter at the third bar, so that the trumpet briefly provides an obbligato. At the end a *Dal segno* provides the postlude. Example 71 shows the part for first trumpet in the prelude, for Bach's setting of the *Passion Chorale*.

Bach very rarely used horns as obbligato instruments against a chorale melody. In the opening chorus of his *Cantata 128*, "Auf Christi Himmelfahrt allein," the sopranos sing the chorale melody as a *cantus firmus*. The horns in G assume the clarino function, with parts that are rhythmic, florid, and imitative. Example 72 gives the second phrase of this setting, in which the first horn reaches d''' and the second horn c'''.

In the first movement of Bach's *Cantata 80*, "Ein' feste Burg," the first trumpet takes over the function performed by the soprano in Example 72. (In the Library of Congress there is a manuscript *contrafactum* of this movement, with the words "Gaudete omnes populi." This arrangement, there ascribed to G. H. Stölzel (!), is identical with a version in Friedemann Bach's handwriting that was at one time in the Berlin National Library.) Here the voices, supported by strings, develop in highly polyphonic fashion the successive phrases of "Ein' feste Burg." Each phrase is climaxed by the soaring notes of the stately chorale theme itself, played by the trumpet, with the support of unison oboes an octave lower. As a crowning Bach cachet, there is a canon at the distance of a bar and three octaves apart, between the trumpet and the continuo. In the eighth phrase Bach has written the rare g#″ for the trumpet. The reader is urged to examine this entire movement, as it is printed in Jahrgang XVIII of the *Bachgesellschaft Edition.*

iv.   Brass License

Because of their incomplete scale in the lower register, brass instruments have been allowed greater freedom in partwriting than voices or other orchestral instruments. At its simplest, this consists of nothing more than irregular progressions of notes that conventionally resolve in a particular way—suspensions, sevenths, neighboring notes. Here the clashes, if any, are no greater than those which often occur when the brass is not playing, clashes which are the result of the simultaneous occurrence of two or more nonharmonic tones, such as the quadruple appoggiatura with semitonal resolutions in the Allegro molto movement of Mozart's famous *G minor Symphony.* (Example 73) A similar type of clash is the "Corelli cadence" with parallel seconds, the result of a resolving suspension in the upper voice and an anticipation in the lower. The example shown (Example 74) is from

Ex. 73   Ex. 74

Flute, Clarinets I, II, Bassoon I   Violins

Corelli's *Chamber Sonata in D minor*, Opus 2, No. 2. This movement, an Allemande, contains three other such cadences, and they can be found in the Corrente and Giga also.

A frequent license that does not offend the ear when the brass plays is in a cadence which has a 4-3 suspension, such as Example 61. Here, counting repeats, there are eight phrases in which the penultimate chord is ornamented with the suspension. Kuhnau has sidestepped the issue by having the second horn play a fifth with the first horn at each of these cadences. But Bach, in his setting of this same chorale (Example 63), has given the suspended tonic note to the second horn each time the cadence occurs. This is quite clear in the last two cadences, where the c″ is tied from the second to the third beat. Bach's octave leap intensifies the dissonance, the progression normally having the c″ proceed directly to the g′. The brass license consists in having the horn leap to the g′, while the alto voice is resolving the suspension by step, as in Example 61. There might be a leap from c″ to g′ also if the chord in question were a ii₇ or a II₇, chords in which the c″ would usually resolve on b′. Or perhaps the c″ might be a passing note in the voice part, in the sequence d″ c″ b′ c″, and here too the second horn would play the g′ instead of the seldom used b′.

Actual clashes between the brass and other instruments and voices are probably as old as the employment of trumpets in art music. It is easy to imagine the trumpet that played "In dulci jubilo" in Example 14 or the coachhorn that played "Lieber Joseph" in Example 15—it is easy to imagine them playing along with other instruments that were less limited in scale than they were. The result? Some parts that coincided beautifully; some parts that did not coincide, but happened to harmonize; some parts that clashed badly because the intervals were seconds.

Two early seventeenth-century German composers trained in the multiple-choir technique of the Venetian school illustrate the waywardness of the trumpet writing at that time. Heinrich Schütz, having learned this Venetian technique directly from Giovanni Gabrieli, applied it in various works, including a setting of *Psalm 136* for obbligato trumpet and thirteen voice parts in three choirs. (The voices in the second choir were doubled by trombones.) The C trumpet was assigned three successive motives. The second of these motives rises to d″ and e″, but the first and third lie wholly within the arpeggio or coachhorn range of the instrument—c′, e′, g′, c″. Thus, with many repetitions of the arpeggio motive, almost in passacaglia style, clashes were almost bound to arise. Example 75 is taken from the third and final section of *Psalm 136*, with the voice parts being severely compressed. Although the harmony in these four bars consists of nothing but tonic and dominant triads, the trum-

Ex. 75

pet's c′ or c″ boldly clashes four times with the dominant harmony and its e′ clashes with it twice.

To prove that Schütz's independent trumpet was no personal
caprice, we have Michael Praetorius' setting of "In dulci jubilo"
for four trumpets and sixteen voices in four choirs. Praetorius
learned from Schütz the art of writing for multiple choirs, and
may have learned from him also how to write freely for trumpets.
At any rate, although the first two trumpets are harmonious, save
for a couple of imitative parts for the second trumpet, the third
(Principal oder Quinta) and fourth (Alter Bass) trumpets pay
little attention to the underlying harmony. Thus e′ and g′ clash
with the subdominant triad, c′ and e′ with the dominant. Example

Ex. 76 (a)

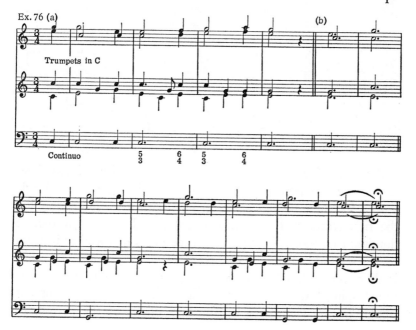

76 (a) gives the four trumpets and the continuo in the first phrase in which they appear, and (b) the last two phrases of the setting. (The note values have been reduced four times.) Note that in bar six of (b) it is the imitating second trumpet that is out of step with the harmony.

The Overture to Steffani's opera, *Niobe* (Munich, 1688) has some outrageously clashing dissonance for trumpets also. In the form of a French overture, the Grave is for strings only. In the fugued Allegro, four trumpets and timpani are added, with fugal rhythmic patterns of their own. There are so many passing chords formed by the strings that it is often difficult to state what the essential harmony is. But one may safely say that the trumpets' c′ clashes with dominant and mediant harmony, e′ with dominant and subdominant, and g′ with subdominant. Example 77 is taken from the latter part of the Allegro, starting with bar 22; it shows many of the clashes.

Ex. 77

Trumpets in C

Strings

Bach and Handel have provided many exciting brass dissonances. In the latter's *Occasional Oratorio* there is a Marche scored for three trumpets and strings, with first violins doubling the first trumpet. In the phrase cited in Example 78 there is dominant harmony for the first three beats of the first bar; but on the second beat the second trumpet plays a concert f♯′ which is alien to the chord. Here, as often, the fifth partial (e′) is used as a leaping lower neighbor to the sixth partial (g′). This particular license seemed to be almost a cliché of the period, for

Ex. 78

Trumpets in D (Concert Notation)

Strings

Bach has used it in the final cadences of all three of his wedding chorales. (Vol. 13 of the *Bachgesellschaft Edition*.)

At the beginning of the second bar of Handel's Marche the viola plays b′, a note of the expected strong supertonic triad; but the third trumpet negates the b′ by sounding a′. On the last beat of this bar, the second trumpet leaps from a′ to d″, although the harmony does not change from the dominant, A major. Then, on the last beat of the third bar, the trumpets and the bass spell out a submediant seventh, a satisfactory chord at this point; but the viola's g′ makes the harmony in the strings a subdominant triad. So, in this one phrase, Handel has allowed his trumpets to clash with the strings in five ways: c″ against the dominant, e′ against the dominant and subdominant, and g′ against the subdominant and supertonic.

Bach has more than matched Handel's licenses with brass instruments. The *First Brandenburg Concerto* has the most concentrated assemblage of wayward notes for horns. In the opening ritornello of the first movement there is a cadence in which the harmonic progression is vi IV vii⁰ I V I. Not only is there a rhythmic clash here, as elsewhere in the movement, between the triplet eighths of the horns and the sixteenths in the strings, but the horns sound a written g′ against IV, c″ against vii⁰, and, worst of all, e′ against V—thus completely refuting the cadence so clearly presented in the strings. (Example 79 (a))

A similar refutation occurs at the final cadence of the movement in ⁶⁄₈ meter (and also earlier in the movement), where the strings present another normal cadence: I vi ii₇ V I. Here the written e′ in the second horn is not obtrusive until the penultimate dominant chord, which it effectually contradicts. (Example

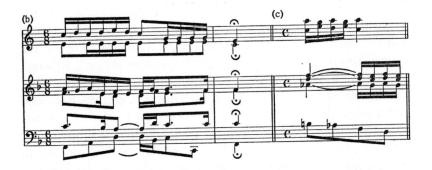

79 (b)) Another clash, involving e″, occurs in the first movement of this concerto, where it is sounded with diminished-
seventh string harmony; the second horn's concert a′ against
the viola's ab′ gives a veritable blues effect! (Example 79 (c)) It
was the licenses in the *First Brandenburg Concerto* which first
directed my attention to brass dissonance, and they continue to
astonish me, since they occur at critical cadential points.

The intruding e′ or e″ in cadential dominant harmony, as in
the Bach examples just shown, was sufficiently common at Bach's
time to raise the question: may at least some of these penultimate
chords be explained as dominant thirteenths? My answer might
have been a resounding No were it not for a cadence in a *German Dance in C* by Mozart. (Example 80) Here the piccolo
melody strongly suggests the progression I V I. The trumpets
play an octave, c′ c″, in the first bar; but on the third beat of
the second bar they play e′ g′, followed by c′ e′ on the next beat.
Also the timpani play G and c on these two beats, repeating these

notes as the trumpets repeat their figure. Certainly the harmony here is not iii I, is it? But to my way of thinking, a dominant thirteenth would be valid as a hypothesis only when the fifth is absent from the dominant chord, as in the Mozart example. In the Bach examples (Examples 79 (a) and (b)) the fifth is present.

Ex. 80

Piccolo

Trumpets in C

In the National Library in Vienna there are six collections of minuets by Franz Asplmayr (there are half a dozen variant spellings of his name), with eighty minuets in all. These are scored mostly for oboes, horns, and strings, without violas. All are extremely boring, as if written between beers. (Asplmayr was born in 1721, eleven years before Haydn.) In one set of twelve minuets, seven of the first eight show an odd cliché at the end of the first section. A dominant cadence is made in the last two bars of the section, during which the horns play g' and d'', the root and fifth of the dominant triad. In three of the minuets the cadential formula (in the dominant key) is I V I; in three others, ii I V I; in *Menuetto No. 4*, IV I V I. Examples 81 (a), (b), and (c) show these cadential formulas, not the actual notes in any

Ex. 81 (a)   (b)   (c)

Horns

Cadential formulas

one minuet. By straining a point, one might consider the first of these formulas an example of pedalpoint, although the cadence is not reached until the second bar. But this explanation would hardly serve in the other two formulas, where the progression begins with a chord other than the tonic. These clashes are equivalent to c′ against the dominant triad, g′ against the sub-dominant, and both c′ and g′ against the supertonic.

For completeness' sake let us examine one phrase in the Menuetto of Mozart's *Musikalischer Spass* for horns and string quartet. (Example 82) The horns in F play sequential thirds, while the viola and 'cello also play in thirds, doubled in the higher

Ex. 82

Horns in F

Viola and 'Cello, doubled in higher octave by Violins I and II

octave by the violins. If there were no accidentals in the horn parts, the harmony would be impeccable. But Mozart's "joke" at this point consists in having the horns play notes which are altered by stopping. Even so, it is not until the third bar that the concert f♯′ in the second horn clashes badly with the f of the viola and the f′ of the first violin. In the fourth bar, the concert c♯′ in the second horn clashes with the c of the 'cello and the c′ of the second violin. But these sophisticated clashes that simulate the unskilled playing of village musicians have no connection whatever with the other clashes shown in this chapter, clashes which involve the fourth, fifth, sixth, and eighth notes of the harmonic series.

The amazing thing to note about these "other" clashes is that the great majority of them did *not* occur because the unfortunate composer could not help himself, because he had no better notes to use in the lower range. We have seen how much both Bach and Handel enjoyed using the *clarino* range for both trumpets and horns. By writing higher notes they could easily have avoided any of the clashes shown in our examples. It is true that sometimes leaps were used instead of stepwise passing or neighboring notes, and would be heard as legitimate nonharmonic tones. But Steffani's *Niobe* experiments, which should be quoted *in extenso* for their proper appreciation, and the cadences in the *First Brandenburg Concerto* seem to reveal a definite opposition between two planes of harmony. A fundamental difference between brass and strings, involving both their tone color and traditional function, appeared to be part of the thinking of the eighteenth-century composer. And so a clash arising from a fanfare did not have to be explained by learned talk about secondary seventh chords, about dominant ninths and thirteenths, or about pedals, appoggiaturas and anticipations. It was enough to say that the trumpet or horn was playing.

After seeing—and hearing—the examples in this section, one becomes conscious of the fact that Beethoven's famous false entrance of the second horn in the first movement of the *Eroica Symphony* was quite mild, after all. (Example 83) There the clash was that of e′ against dominant harmony, actually only against the seventh of a dominant seventh, the third and fifth being absent from the chord. Compared with Bach and Handel, Steffani and Asplmayr, this is pretty small potatoes!

Ex. 83

CHAPTER III

Horns in the Symphony

❧

i. Horn versus Trumpet

As we have seen, the foundation of trumpet style was the military signal, in which repeated notes were prominent, including the dactylic rhythmic motive of an eighth and two sixteenths. If arpeggio melody, even in the higher octave, was also present, this was a sure sign of brass style. The *clarino* style, superimposed upon the more obvious fanfare, consisted of florid melody in the higher octave, moving largely by step. It was ordinarily a *moto perpetuo* in sixteenth notes, and the second trumpet, if playing, was often a third lower then the first trumpet, but might go above it if the melody in the first trumpet went below e″. Octaves were common, especially with arpeggio melody, and in the cadence the octave, c′-c″, was favored over the sixth, e′-c″.

It is too much to say that orchestral horn style was based upon hunting calls, as the trumpet style was based upon military signals. Although "la Chasse" in $\frac{6}{8}$ meter was a favorite concluding movement of a symphony, and entire symphonies as well were based on hunting calls (see the last section of this chapter), this was not the predominant or even the essential feature of horn style. What *was* characteristic of the horns in the hunting movements was what has been termed the "horn progression," the notes c″, d″, e″ in the first horn, with e′, g′, and c″ in the second. Even without the $\frac{6}{8}$ meter, these three melody notes in any order or rhythm will be regarded as horn melody—provided they are accompanied by the proper lower notes. This horn progression

84

was the foundation of the important, but, for the players, often dull, accompanying function of the horns, as in the operas of Gluck, the Mannheim symphonies, and the Classic symphony in general.

Very often, when the horns and trumpets were playing together, the horns doubled the trumpets an octave lower, as in Pichl's octave fanfare in Example 23. (The text there made references also to Mozart and to both Joseph and Michael Haydn.) Handel made a practice of such doubling, as in four choruses of his *Joshua*. With Handel the style of the doubled parts is trumpet style, and so is it at the beginning of the Finale of a Haymann *Oboe Concerto in C*, with the bold octaves and syncopation. (Example 84) In the minuet of a Zimmermann

Ex. 84

Trumpets in C, doubled by Horns

Symphony in C (T.&T. 1), however, the style is purely that of the horns; so that it would be proper to say that here the trumpets double the horns instead of vice versa. (Example 85)

The horn style is predominant in the *Choral Symphony*, and Beethoven makes his trumpets humbly tag along. Note especially

Ex. 85

Horns in C, doubled by Trumpets

the orchestral presentation of the Joy Theme in the Finale, with trumpets in D being doubled by horns in D. (Example 86) This theme, by the way, was chosen by the great Harvard mathematician, George D. Birkhoff, as the perfect melody, the touchstone by which all other melodies are to be judged. (See his *Aesthetic Measure*.) But, in my opinion, the Joy Theme is more stupid and banal than the most trivial folksong that Beethoven might have chosen in its stead. (The Joy Theme has even permeated our churches, thanks to Henry Van Dyke's "Joyful, joyful, we adore Thee," a text worthy of the tune!) As horn melody, however, the Joy Theme assumes a different aspect.

The melody fits the pair of horns like a glove. To be sure, this had become an archaic horn style a half century before the post-Napoleonic era in which the *Ninth Symphony* was conceived. Taken as the apotheosis of the horn idiom of Gluck and the *Chasse*, as a stupendous horn duet, accompanied by orchestra and chorus,—from such a viewpoint the principal theme of the Finale of the *Choral Symphony* begins to make sense.

Ex. 86

There is another place where Beethoven has caught the inner spirit of the horns: in the Allegro of his *Fifth Piano Concerto* in E flat. In the first exposition, the solo horns, *dolce*, play a square-cut little phrase, part of the second subject. (Example 87) In the second exposition the motive appears in the dominant key, and then again in E flat in the recapitulation, with full orchestra, although the octave trumpets are assigned their not uncommon rôle in Beethoven's music, the Cinderella rôle of doubling the timpani. This motive recurs in the Coda, where it is played by

Ex. 87

the horns, with piano figuration and string punctuation. To me there is something magical about these passages, although the material upon which they are based is the most hackneyed sort of horn melody.

When the horns were not actually doubling the trumpets, they would often play in a wholly similar style, as in a passage from the chorus, "Praise the Lord," in Handel's *Solomon*, which could be played well enough on four trumpets, or, for that matter, on four horns. However, the octave separation, as well as the difference in timbre, brings out the imitation between first horn and first trumpet. At the end of this chorus, Handel does make a distinction between the horns and the trumpets, allotting repeated notes and arpeggios to the trumpets, but giving the horns a more sustained part. Were it not for the high tessitura and the weak dominant octave at the final cadence, these horns would have been at home in a symphony of the Classical period. (Examples 88 (a) and (b)) In another chorus in *Solomon*, "From the censer curling," the horns answer the trumpets antiphonally.

Ex. 88 (a)

Trumpets in D (Concert Notation)

Horns in D (Concert Notation)

(b)

In the early symphony there frequently were no trumpets; rarely were there trumpets without horns. A definite horn style evolved in the second half of the eighteenth century, various aspects of which will be discussed in later sections of this chapter. But, while this horn style was evolving, one finds many interesting instances, first, of horns which play in *clarino* style without doubling trumpets, and, later, of trumpets that similarly take over the functions of horns.

A bass solo in Homilius' cantata, *Die Freude der Hirten*, is accompanied by three trumpets and timpani, two oboes, and

strings. But, for the tenor solo, "Die Engel frohlocken," he substituted three horns for the trumpets, and also in the final chorus,
"Heil dem besten Hirten." In the tenor solo the homophonic
horns in G interject a fanfarish motive, which occurs ten times
in all. There is a similar motive in the final chorus, used seven
times. The latter motive takes the first horn to c''', the same
written note which he had to play on the first trumpet in D in
the bass solo. (Examples 89 (a) and (b)) In Zachow's cantata,

Ex. 89 (a)   (b)

Horns in G

"Mein Seel' erhebt den Herren," there is a tenor aria ("Gott
stürzt") in which the horns in F have an almost wholly fanfaring
passage which includes rhythmically repeated notes in *clarino*
style. (Example 90)

Ex. 90

Horns in F

Another aspect of *clarino* melody is present in the Allegro
molto of a Leopold Mozart *Symphony in D* (T.&T.1), where
the first horn sweeps up to f''' in the first of three scalewise melismas. Both horns have a rhythmic motive in the fifth bar of Example 91. Paul Wranitzky, a generation later than Leopold (he

Ex. 91

Horns in D

was born in 1756, the same year as Wolfgang), wrote conventionally for both horns and trumpets. But at the end of the first movement of his *Symphony in D*, Opus 36, his first horn engages in
flourishes that go up to e'''. (Example 92) Since neither the horns
nor the trumpets go higher than g'' in ten other Wranitzky sym-

phonies which I have examined, this sudden fanfare is perplexing
in the extreme.

Examples are not lacking, on the other hand, of trumpets that
were treated more or less like horns. In the Allegro assai of a
Richter *Symphony in D* (T.&T.6), for example, the "horn

Ex. 92

1st Horn in D

progression" is present in a passage for trumpets. But only a
couple of bars later, the trumpets are polyphonic, as only
trumpets properly were! (Examples 93 (a) and (b)) An even
smaller print of the horn, this time principally of the second horn,
occurs in the Allegro moderato of a Fiala *Symphony in C* (T.&T.
2), in a passage which begins with characteristic *clarino* octave
arpeggios, but ends with the swift arpeggio descent in the second

Ex. 93 (a)

Trumpets in D

(b)

trumpet that has been written so often for second horn. (Example 94) Trumpets also play in the Trio of the minuet of
Riepel's *Quodlibeticum in D* (T.&T.19), but horns would have
given the passage a more convincing ring. In the "Dona nobis"
of Haydn's *Missa in Tempore Belli* the trumpets likewise attempt

Ex. 94

Trumpets in C

the *pas de menuet* and a *faux pas* it really is! (Example 95) There
is a similar horn-like phrase for trumpets in the "Et vitam ven-
turi" of his *Missa Sanctae Ceciliae*.

A strong indication of the ambiguous state of the brass in the
middle of the 18th century is found in a Wagenseil *Symphony in
D*, 1746, printed in the *Austrian Denkmäler* (XV²[31]), where

the parts are listed as for horns *or* trumpets. This suggests the possibility of the music being played by an orchestra into which horns had not yet been introduced, or by an orchestra in which a single pair of players would perform on either trumpets or horns as the occasion arose.

Ex. 95

Trumpets in C

In a number of works in the Thurn and Taxis Library there are similar indications with respect to the brass. In a Bernasconi *Symphony in D* (T.&T.1) for horns and strings, a copyist has added on the parts "Clarino o Cornu." (This is the only one of six symphonies in this library allegedly by Bernasconi which is not really by Pokorny.) In Bonno's *Symphony in D* (T.&T.1; the two other Bonno symphonies are really by Pokorny) there are both horns and trumpets in the score. The trumpets, which are less interesting than the horns in the first and last movements of the symphony, shine in the Trio of the minuet, the horns being silent. This was a wildly improbable scoring in any symphony of this period, where the horns dominated, and one can understand why someone has interchanged the names "Corno" and "Clarino" on the parts. Again, in the first of three *Symphonies in D* by Guiseppe Scarlatti in the Thurn and Taxis Library, the parts are listed on the cover as horns and strings, but "Clarino" is written on the parts themselves, although these are typical accompanying horn parts. Very similar parts are in Schiebl's trivial and Italianate *Symphony in C* (T.&T.1), where they are called "Clarini" only.

A similar confusion of brass parts exists in three oboe concerti by Pachschmidt in the Thurn and Taxis Library. Here, according to the score, the solo oboe is to be accompanied by *clarini* and strings. In the opening ritornello of the first concerto (T.&T.25,1763) the *clarini* are prominent. Although the style is not decisively that of either horn or trumpet, the fact that the brass are opposed to the principal motive in the violins suggests that a much better balance would be obtained if the parts were being played by horns an octave lower. This belief is confirmed in the other two concerti, where someone has written "Corni" over "Clarini" in the score and where the parts (which have disappeared for the first concerto) read "Cornu I" and "Cornu II."

A final bit of confusion is to be found in two works by Zach in the Thurn and Taxis Library. In a *Sinfonie Concertante in D* (T.&T.7) for violin, with *clarinetti, corni,* and strings, the excitement which one might feel at discovering clarinet parts in a work by Zach (1699-1773) is dissipated when one examines the parts and discovers that they are really *clarini* parts, almost identical with those of the *corni,* but not playing so much. Zach also has a *Flute Concerto in G* (T.&T.16), the accompaniment being provided by "Clarinetti obligatti" and strings. But here the parts are marked "Cornu primo" and "Cornu 2do," and horn parts they really are. Zach's misuse of the word "clarinetti" suggests that the four concertos of his contemporay, J. M. Molter, for "clarinetto concertato" (Das Erbe deutscher Musik, Band 41) may also have been intended for an instrument other than the clarinet. Except for an occasional c', e' or g', these concertos contain no note for the solo instrument lower than c''.

ii.   Allegro Horn Melody

During the second half of the eighteenth century a definite style emerged for the first horn, the *cor-alto.* Although this style was most characteristic in fast movements, as in the first or last movements of a symphony, it was not uncommon in slow movements and minuets. The first-horn style was compounded of many elements, including some that more properly belonged to the trumpet, such as the octave arpeggios that Johann Stamitz delighted to write for trumpets and horns or for horns alone. See, for example, the opening flourish in the Allegro molto of a Stamitz *Symphony in F* (DTB F3), which is scored for oboes, horns, and strings. (Example 96) A similarly scored *Symphony in D* (DTB D12) also begins with an octave fanfare, its tension increased by syncopation. (Example 97) In another *Symphony*

Ex. 96

Horns in F

in D (DTB D8), with both trumpets and horns in the score, the latter play higher and more often, as in the Presto movement, where horn octaves introduce the fragment shown and also emphasize its ending. (Example 98) No other composer of the eighteenth century could rival the nervous excitement engendered by the tremendous sweep of Stamitz's horn parts. But

Ex. 97

Horns in D

the other composers could not help being influenced by these parts.

Fanfare melody for horns without octave doubling also occurred with some frequency, although not always in Allegros. There will be examples later in this chapter, in the discussion of

Ex. 98

Horns in D

the minuet and the *chasse*. In Allegro movements the fanfares were rather more common at the beginning or the ending, to give added emphasis at these points. For example, a Sandel *Symphony in D* (T.&.T.5) begins with a flourish in triple meter for unison horns. (Example 99) Punto, likewise, begins his *Tenth Horn Concerto* in F with a five-bar fanfare.

Ex. 99

Horns in D

The fanfares might occur even more appropriately in a coda, as in the Overture to Traetta's opera, *Ippolito ed Aricia*, where the second horn plays in harmony with the first. (Example 100) The concert notation for the key of D was not uncommon

Ex. 100

Horns in D

among the Italian opera composers, as we have indicated in Chapter 1. Near the end of the Allegro moderato of Punto's *Seventh Horn Concerto* in F the horn indulges in some animated flourishes, with triplet sixteenths. But Punto's flourishes are more than matched in the Allegro of Danzi's *Concertante in E flat* (T.&T.3), where the solo horn touches c''' and where the quintuplets give added spice. (Example 101)

Ex. 101

Horns in Eb

We conclude the illustrations of horn fanfares with two examples from the great Classic masters. In the Allegro of Haydn's *Symphony No. 13* in D the four horns play a unison fanfare, with arresting effect. (Example 102) Then, in Mozart's *Marriage of Figaro*, the horns jeer at Figaro, as he dolefully sings about the duplicity of women in the aria, "Aprite un po' quegli occhi."

Ex. 102

Four Horns in D

There is nothing unusual about this little passage, except that it is more trumpet-like than horn-like and that it bursts forth most unexpectedly. This is Mozart's famous musical pun about poor Figaro, who was afraid he might wear the cuckold's horns before he wore a wedding ring. (Example 103)

Ex. 103

ff
Horns in Eb

Although both the fanfare and the florid scale passage were elements taken over from the *clarino* idiom, it was the latter that provided the basis for what was to become an idiomatic horn style. See, for example, a scale passage in the Allegro of a Rosetti *Horn Concerto in E flat*, which covers the range from g' to d''', including two mildly stopped notes, a' and b'. (Example 104)

These two bars are then repeated immediately. We have already noted in Example 91 Leopold Mozart's contribution to floridity in the acute register and Pokorny's in Example 58—both have f''' for the top note.

But a horn part did not have to lie in the *clarino* register in order to have the benefits of *clarino* floridity. By a judicious in-

Ex. 104

Horns in Eb

sertion of stopped notes, an interesting melodic line could be written with much stepwise movement, but with a comparatively low tessitura. In Mozart's *First Horn Concerto* in D, the first movement ends with a brilliant passage for the horn, which lies entirely between g' and g''. In addition to the common a' and b', the passage has four stopped c♯''. (Example 105) Although

Ex. 105

Horn in D

Haydn's well-known *Trumpet Concerto in E flat* was written for a keyed trumpet, most of it could have been played on a horn, using stopped notes, and other passages were not beyond the capabilities of an ordinary trumpet. There is one little florid passage in the first movement which either trumpet or horn could have performed with ease, for it rose only to the fourteenth harmonic, bb'', and had no notes foreign to the harmonic series save the generally accepted neighboring note b'. When the passage first occurs, the quarters, g'' and f'', are present; the continuous pattern of sixteenths comes later in the movement, where the passage ends with the c'' in the third bar. The sixteenths, g'' and f'', shown in parenthesis, also belong to the second version. (Example 106)

But floridity alone was not enough to ensure interest; the variety of rhythm in the Mozart excerpt (Example 105) makes it more pleasing than the passage from Haydn (Example 106). Rosetti, whose brilliant style has already been illustrated in Example 104, has also shown how brilliance can be incorporated in a musically satisfying melodic line. In another Rosetti *Horn Concerto in Eb* (Krul 3b/11), the Allegro spiritoso movement contains as part of the second subject a passage that has almost exactly the same compass as the former example, g'-c''' compared

Ex. 106

Keyed Trumpet in Eb

to g'-d'''. But here the continuous pattern of sixteenths breaks off after the first bar, and in bars four and five lasts for only half a bar. There are no fanfares; but the drop of a seventh at bar six dramatically underscores the approaching dominant cadence. (Example 107)

Ex. 107

Horn in Eb

Among the eighteenth-century concertos for horn or trumpet there were few that contained the *moto perpetuo* type of brass floridity which is so common in the musically worthless compositions turned out today for the ambitious young player on cornet or euphonium. A brazen exception was the Minuetto cantabile con variationi that concluded Punto's *Eleventh Horn Concerto* in E. This illustrious hornist was a great master of effects, but had a very slender talent as a composer. These variations all contain hackneyed arpeggios in keyboard style: the first has triplet eighths; the second, a rhythm of four thirty-seconds and an eighth; the third alternates eighths with paired sixteenths; the fourth is wholly in sixteenths. (Example 108) Surely Punto's virtuosity was misplaced in such unidiomatic figuration!

In addition to the floridity and flourishes borrowed from *clarino* style, the melodic character of the eighteenth-century horn was often straightforward and unpretentious, as in the horn

parts in G for Handel's chorus, "See, the conquering hero comes," in *Judas Maccabaeus*. (Example 109) The march-like squareness of the Handel chorus can be matched in a chorus from Rameau's motet, "Diligam te, Domine," where the horns

deport themselves much as they might in a bourrée or gavotte. (Example 110)

In the Allegro of Punto's *Eleventh Horn Concerto* in E there is bourrée melody. (Example 111) Then, in the duple-meter Trio for horns in F and unison oboes in the Polacca of Bach's

First Brandenburg Concerto, the horns play what is practically gavotte melody. (Example 112) In all four of the above examples there is strong and regular accentuation and a smoothly flowing melody.

Of course, there were melodic and strongly accented trumpet

marches coeval with the horn marches. There is, for example, a passage in the Chor der Helden of Telemann's *Trauercantata*, where convincing bourrée melody is presented by three trumpets, grouped antiphonally. (Example 113) If one seeks a prototype for lyricism allied to marching rhythm, it can be found in Fan-

tini's *Balletto detto l'Alsani* for trumpet and continuo. (Example 114. The bass part is written an octave high for the sake of convenience.) But, broadly speaking, throughout the eighteenth century this type of melody belonged particularly to the horn rather than to the trumpet.

Lyric melody unassociated with dance rhythms was the special province of Pokorny in the parts which he wrote for first horn. But these high and eloquent melodies were almost always associated with a contrasted part for second horn. There are two especially good specimens which occur in Allegro assai movements of Pokorny *Symphonies in E flat* (T.&T.91, 92), which are erroneously ascribed to Monn. In the latter (Example 115) there are little motives in eighths and triplet eighths in the first horn which are imitated by the second horn; in addition the second horn

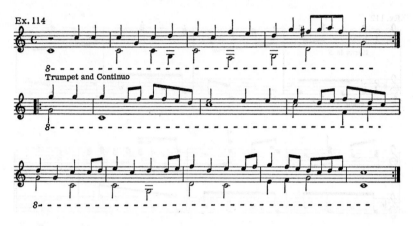

Ex. 114

has four groups of descending arpeggios, and plays some low notes.

Since the second horn, in its most servile limitation to a low tessitura, played nothing but arpeggio melody, it is not strange that the fanfare type of melody should remain prominent among the devices that comprised the second-horn style. These fanfares were often an earmark rather than an integral part of second-horn melody, an amusing little flourish in the midst of more

Ex. 115

sedate movement. Some of these occur in examples shown later in this chapter, such as the arpeggios in a minuet Trio of a Pokorny symphony (Example 144) and the six-note flourish in the Adagio of a Krommer *Harmoniemusik.* (Example 217)

In the first Allegro assai in E flat, Pokorny exploits the arpeggios for second horn and also allots the first horn some melismas. (Example 116) But in an Allegro movement of a *Symphony in D* (T.&T.31) the first horn is as calm as an arpeggio ascent to e''' allows him to be, while the second horn has wide-

Ex. 116

Horns in Eb

spread tonic and dominant broken chords in sixteenths, including a hazardous f#' as a lower neighbor. (Example 117)

Examples 115 and 116 contain a few triplet eighths, used melodically. Arpeggiated triplet eighths for the second horn were a sure Pokorny trademark, as in the Allegro of still another *Symphony in E flat* (T.&T. 87), where the leaps for second horn include a fourteenth and where the first horn gradually ascends to f'''. (Example 118) (This symphony also appears as Pokorny

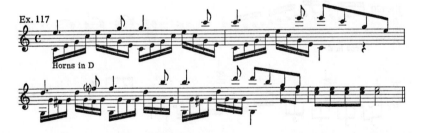

Ex. 117

Horns in D

95.) The overwhelming evidence of a unified Pokorny horn style, as shown here and elsewhere in this book, corroborates the documentary evidence that he was the true composer of all the symphonies to which a score of other composers' names had also been assigned.

Ex. 118

Horns in Eb

In the Beethoven *Sextet* from which a passage of horn thirds
has been culled (Example 48), a seventeen-note gradually descending fanfare for second horn is immediately followed by a
twelve-note ascending scale for first horn, an illustration in miniature of the contrasting horn styles. (Example 119) But the
choicest epitome of the Allegro style for horns occurs in an

Ex. 119

Horns in Eb

eight-bar period in the first movement of a Schacht *Double Concerto in E*. (Example 120) The first horn begins with a florid
sweep inherited from *clarino* technique. Next, both horns play
sighing appoggiaturas in thirds. Then, while the first horn majes-
tically attains g''' (concert b''), the second horn busies himself
with a brilliant fanfare. The passage ends lyrically. Much later
than Pokorny or Schacht, Franz Krommer was to exploit to the
full this more lyric style for horns, liberally buttressed with
stopped notes. (See Examples 203 and 217.)

Ex. 120

Horns in E

If it appears from the above examples that the solo performer
on the *cor-basse* required better technique than his companion
on the *cor-alto*, the supposition is correct. The *primo* hornist had
to be able to reach extremely high notes upon occasion; he had
to have command of a facile technique for the florid passages;
he had to have good control to play lyrically at a high tessitura.
The *secondo* hornist needed a facile technique also, to play the
arpeggios in fast notes, much more hazardous because of their
leaps than the scalewise movement in the first horn. He had to
be able to change registers quickly; he was sometimes assigned

scale passages also, and these might require stopping; he might even have to play tricky high notes.

Some of the difficulties which a *ripieno* second hornist had to face in the latter part of the eighteenth century are shown in the Poco Adagio of a Maschek *Parthia in E flat.* (Example 121)

Ex. 121

(There is an uncertainty as to whether this was by Vincenz or Paul Maschek. However, of the four Maschek symphonies at the Thurn and Taxis Library, two have hopelessly dull parts, the third is more interesting—rightly so, since it is really by Pokorny, and this Parthia, the fourth, has the most interesting horn parts of all. The very active second horn in it suggests Pokorny as the composer; the stopped notes point rather in the direction of Schacht. In any case, I doubt whether we should worry whether it is by Vincenz or by Paul.) In the fourth bar the second horn plays an octave scale, topping it with c'''—the very note, concert eb'', that is so often muffed today by a *primo* hornist in the Scherzo of the *Eroica Symphony*. The arpeggio that follows ends on the second harmonic, c, three octaves lower than c'''. Meanwhile the first horn has a routine part, with a bit of stopping for d#'' (eb''), and even his fanfare at the end of the passage is doubled in the lower octave by the more trustworthy second horn!

iii.   Second Subject

In a Sonata-Allegro movement of the early symphony, the horns often had significant melodic functions in the first subject. For contrast they might be silent during the second subject. But, when they did play in the second subject, a problem arose because of the limitations of scale. If the first horn played a melodic part in the dominant key in the exposition, this might well be out of range if transposed a fourth higher in the reprise; if transposed a fifth lower, some unplayable notes were almost sure to be present.

A good solution to the problem posed by the transposed second subject was to give the horns characteristic melodic fragments only in the reprise, motives which they could easily play in the tonic key. Thus, in the reprise of the Allegro con brio movement of Schmidt's *Sinfonie Periodique No. 2 in G*, the horns join the other instruments in arpeggio flourishes which they did not play and could not have played in the dominant key in the exposition. Similarly, in the Presto Finale of a Hoffmeister *C major Symphony* (1780), the second subject is allotted to the strings in the exposition, with oboe doubling later; in the reprise the horns and oboes share the second subject. In a Pachschmidt *Symphony in G* (T.&T.7) there is a passage in the second subject in the exposition in which the horns have a simple accompanying figure on the dominant chord; at the corresponding place in the reprise the horns, in thirds, are given the melody. The fourteen-year-old Mozart contributed a charming example of changed instrumentation in his soprano aria, "Per pietà, bell' idol mio," (K78). The accompaniment is for oboes, horns, and strings. At one point the florid vocal line in the dominant key is followed a third lower by the oboe. Later the passage recurs a fifth lower, in the tonic key, with the first horn taking over the oboe's rôle.

Of course, the horns sometimes did make the transposition to the higher fourth in the reprise, as in a Christian Cannabich *Symphony in D* (T.&T.12), where a five-note scale figure, g' a' b' c'' d'' is played four times in the exposition, becoming c'' d'' e'' f'' g'' in the reprise. Although Cannabich needed stopped notes for the performance of his little figure in the exposition, Friedemann Bach managed without them in his *Concerto for Two Harpsichords* in E flat. In the second subject of the first movement, the trumpets, doubled by the horns, play in a fairly high range in the dominant key in the exposition, but the passage is so written that no stopped notes are needed when it is lowered a fifth in the reprise. (Example 122)

Where the horns had a more humdrum part to play, the problem of the second subject was less acute. In Neth's *Symphony in* G, for example, the horns are given a completely menial rôle, as harmonic support. In the first movement, the exposition and the reprise end with identical harmony, in the dominant and tonic key respectively: i VI IV♭ IV♯ I V♯ I. The trivial horn passages here are sufficiently alike to be accepted as the same.

Ex. 122 (a)   (b)

Trumpets in Eb, doubled by Horns

The repetition of the same rhythm in the reprise might be enough to suggest complete correspondence of horn parts. Friedemann Bach's brother, Johann Christian, for example, assigned a typical horn motive to horns and oboes in the second subject of the first movement of his *E flat Symphony*, Op. 9, No. 2. When this motive returned in the tonic key in the reprise, it had the same rhythm and the same range, but an altered melody. Since the notes played by the strings just before and after this motive are identical, save for key, in exposition and reprise, the listener would undoubtedly have accepted the entire section as the transposed equivalent of what had gone before.

In Haydn's *First Horn Concerto* in D, the J. C. Bach solution is presented on a higher melodic plane. (Example 123) The

Ex. 123 (a)

p
Horn in D

(b)

Adagio is in A, with the solo horn still in D. The quoted part of the second subject, being in the dominant key, is thus in the written key of D for the horn, and lies between d″ and d‴. (The same top note had been approached by leap in the first movement.) In the reprise, this passage, save for the initial g′, lies in approximately the same range as before (d″-b″). The general outline in sufficiently alike and the striking motive of the first two bars is retained. So here also the uncritical ear would accept the two versions as the same.

If the composer had at his command two pairs of brass instruments, crooked in different keys, the problem of the second subject could be easily solved. For example, Leopold Mozart's *Sinfonia da Caccia* in G had two horns in G and two horns in D. The end of the reprise is the exact counterpart of the end of the recapitulation. This fanfare was played at first by the D horns and at the end by the G horns, without changing a note, while the opposite pair of horns gave harmonic punctuation and support. (Example 124)

Ex. 124

Krommer, in the second subject of the first movement of his *First Symphony* in F gave his trumpets in C a motive in octave arpeggios which was then allotted to the horns in F in the reprise. In his much more mature *Fifth Symphony* in E flat, with a full assortment of stopped notes at his disposal, Krommer has written a lovely, romantic passage for the Bb *basso* horns, supported by trombones. The unison Eb horns have a chromatic obbligato part above the Bb horns. (The unison bassoons and third trombone play a staccato bass in quarter notes, not shown in the example.) In the reprise, the Eb horns take over the former notes of the Bb horns *in toto* save for a slight alteration at the cadence. The first Bb horn has assumed the chromatic part of the Eb horns, now written one tone lower and sounding below the principal part instead of above it. (Example 125)

In the first movement of the *Ninth Symphony*, Beethoven has taken excellent advantage of the fact that he has two horns in D and two in Bb *basso*. In the *tutti* near the beginning of the movement, the D horns play the principal motive in the concert key of D minor, resorting to the stopped eb' and eb''. A little later this passage returns in B flat major, with the Bb horns playing the same notes formerly played by the D horns except they are all open. In the second subject in B flat, the horns in B flat play a *dolce* phrase that is brought back in D in the reprise by the D horns. (Example 126) Beethoven has done a somewhat similar thing near the end of his overture, *König Stephan*, which is in E

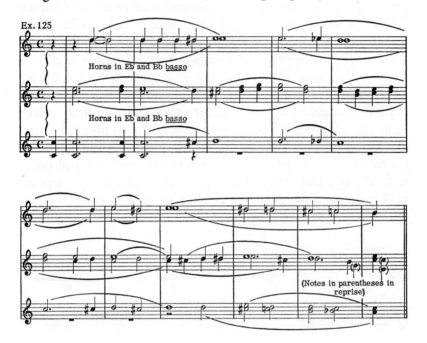

Ex. 125

Horns in Eb and Bb basso

Horns in Eb and Bb basso

(Notes in parentheses in reprise)

flat. The notes played by his horns in C in an eleven-bar passage are immediately played a minor third higher by the horns in E flat, the written notes being the same.

With only two horns available, Rosetti, in the Andante of an *E flat Symphony* (DTB 5a), crooked them in F. Since the key

Ex. 126 (a)   (b)

p dolce   *p dolce*
Horns in Bb basso   Horns in D

of this movement was B flat, the horns were able to play an effective solo passage in the dominant key at the end of the first section. They play a similar solo in the middle of the second section. Then, after fifty bars' rest, they play the very passage with which the first section was concluded. But now the key is B flat, and, although there was no indication of change of crook, the players in Vienna have written in pencil above both horn parts, "Ex B."

The change of crook, as in the Rosetti symphony, was a not uncommon expedient for allowing the horns to play in the reprise. As we have shown in the discussion of crooks in Chapter 1, this was more likely to happen in a symphony in a minor key, where the Finale might change to the tonic major, and the horns, previously crooked in the relative major, would find little chance to play. But, after the general use of stopped notes for horns, no problem remained in transposing passages, even in remote keys. For example, take the Allegro maestoso e risoluto movement from Dauprat's *Third Horn Concerto* in B minor, printed by Coar. The second subject is in the written key of C minor for the solo horn in E, and the horn has to play such stopped notes as f', ab', eb'', and ab''. In the reprise, the same passage appears in G minor, and there are just as many stopped notes as before— eb', f♯', a', and eb''. (Example 127)

Ex. 127 (a)

Horn in E

(b)

iv. Andante and Minuet Trio

The least likely place to find interesting horn melody was in the slow movement of a symphony. In the early symphonies that lacked a minuet, the horns were usually silent in the Andante movement, which would be in a contrasting key, often a minor key. This tradition also extended to four-movement symphonies, no matter how scintillating the horns might be in the minuet Trio. When the horns did play in a slow movement, they usually had a completely menial role. But, especially in concertos, there were a few examples of expressive melody, some of it of genuine romantic sheen.

In the Andante of a *Sinfonia Concertino in D* by Albrechts-berger (T.&T.3), there is a brief solo for first horn, part of which is shown in Example 128. The notes slurred in pairs are a

Ex. 128

Horn in D

visible indication that the passage is to be played with expression, just as they are in a Pokorny *Andante in D* (T.&T.176(b)), part of a *Serenade* wrongly attributed to Kohaut. Here the first horn plays an eight-bar period, very Haydnesque, accompanied only by pizzicato bass. (Example 129) This is a rondo theme

Ex. 129

Horn in D

which occurs four times in the course of the movement. With the added richness of an Adagio tempo, the first horn in B♭ *basso* has a solo in a Vandenbroek *Symphony in B flat* (T.&T.3/3).

Ex. 130

Horn in B♭ <u>basso</u>

As shown in Example 130, it must have needed a completely legato style for its proper interpretation.

The three examples just shown of lyric horns in slow movements have used natural notes only. With stopped notes there were additional possibilities for melodic treatment in the lower octave. In Mozart's *Third Horn Concerto* in E flat the Larghetto is in A flat. So the written key for the solo horn will be F, as in the delightful little phrase in Example 131. But the only stopped

Ex. 131

Horn in Eb

note is a'. Gallay's *Second Horn Duo*, given by Coar, is a charming work, with a typical Andante con moto. Here the horns play as simply as in Pokorny's *Andante*. (See Example 129.) The first section is also an eight-bar diatonic period in the tonic key, with a modulation to the dominant at the cadence. Here, however, the first horn plays the stopped notes, f#', a', and b', while the second horn has b, d', f', and a', as well as the pedal note, f. (Example **132**)

Ex. 132

Horns

The horn quartet in the Adagio of Weber's *Freischütz Overture* is so lyric that it has been turned into a hymn tune for the text, "My Jesus, as Thou wilt." Although this passage was very skillfully written for two horns in F and two horns in C, in order to incorporate as many natural notes as possible, there are a few important stopped notes, such as the a' in bar eight and the d#" in bar twelve, both for the first horn in F. (Example 133) Likewise Mendelssohn, in the magic Nocturne (Andante tranquillo) for horn in E, from his incidental music to *Midsummer Night's Dream*, gives the impression of remaining true to the older tradition. At the beginning, shown in Example 134, the horn, accompanied homophonically by two bassoons, does indeed play open notes; but later in the movement there are a few stopped notes— f#', a', c#".

Ex. 133

To see the full possibilities of stopped notes in the presentation of a lovely melody, let us turn to Rosetti's *Double Concerto in F* (or in E, as an extra set of parts suggests). In the Romance (Adagio non tanto) there is a ten-bar period in the written key of C minor, with a modulation to E flat major at the end of the first phrase. (Example 135) In this tender passage the first horn plays only eb'' and ab'' as stopped notes, but the second horn has eb', f', b', and eb''.

Ex. 134

Ex. 135

Horns in F (or E)

If noteworthy melody for horns seldom occurred in the slow movements of symphonies until the general use of stopped notes, the reverse was true of minuet melody. The explanation is simple enough: the tone of the horn in the middle register was an important adjunct to expressive melody, but this register was severely limited in scale before the advent of stopped notes; on the other hand, the brilliance of the *clarino* register was excellently suited to the horn duets found in Trios. Certain composers, such as Gossec, Vanhal, or even Joseph Haydn, whose horn parts, generally speaking, were useful, but dull, sometimes allowed the horns to come to life in the minuet Trios.

Typically, these Trio melodies were smooth and folklike, as in a Dittersdorf *Symphony in G* (Krebs 52). Example 136 quotes

Ex. 136

Horns in G

the beginning of the second section of the Trio. This is the sort of melody we had seen in the Zimmermann minuet shown in Example 85, which he had strangely scored for trumpets as well as horns. Example 56 had presented canonic arpeggios in another Dittersdorf minuet. Somehow, extended fanfares seem out of place in a minuet, although a good instance can be cited from Haydn's *Symphony No. 99* in E flat, where octave trumpets are doubled by octave horns. A short arpeggio motive for horns can be very effective, as in the Trio of Mozart's *Jupiter Symphony*. (Example 137) This was a popular motive, for it appeared also

Ex. 137

Horns in C

in minuets by Karl Stamitz (DTB D 12, *Symphony in D*) and
Pokorny (T.&T.74, *Symphony in F*).

The most striking of these Trio melodies were not only lyric,
but were also pitched very high. Their prototype was the minuet
written by Zelenka while a student of Fux in Vienna, 1717-19.
(It is quoted in Piersig's *Einführung des Hornes*, p. 123.) In the
first section of this minuet the horn in D must ascend to e′′′ in
a passage that artfully combines conjunct with disjunct movement. (Example 138) Johann Stamitz, whose first movements

Ex. 138

Horn in D

featured bold leaps for the brass, preferred a more flowing style
in the ultra-high melodies of his minuets. In the second section
of the Trio in a *Symphony in G* (DTB G 7) one may note a
certain independence of the second horn, a sequence that in-
troduces f♯′′, and a climax on f′′′. (Example 139) This latter note

Ex. 139

Horns in G

on a G horn is concert c′′′, and this, to the best of my knowledge,
was the highest note in absolute pitch written for horn in the
eighteenth century.

The written g′′′ occurred not infrequently, but never for a
horn pitched higher than E flat or E, which would be concert
b♭′′ or b′′. Another excellent example of flowing Trio melody,
from an *E flat Symphony* by Stamitz (DTB Es 6), does have its
skillfully reached climax on g′′′. (Example 140) A Menuetto
Trio in Adam Veichtner's *Simphonie russienne* in C takes the
first horn in C *basso* up to written a′′′, the twenty-sixth or
twenty-seventh harmonic! (Example 141) Unless there is later
evidence to the contrary, this must be considered the highest

Ex. 140

Horns in Eb

harmonic written for the horn, although in absolute pitch it lies
below the g''' on the E-flat or E horn and the f''' on the G horn.
Veichtner has written an interesting melody, with a bold and
independent part for second horn. (Several other symphonies

Ex. 141

Horns in C

by Veichtner which I have examined have horn parts of most
conventional cast. Was there a strange Russian influence that
inspired this brief effulgence? Veichtner had been a violinist
of the Russian Count Kaiserling in Königsberg several years before this symphony was published.)

The redoubtable Pokorny has also displayed his genius in the
horn parts of his minuets. In a *Symphony in G* (T.&T.15) the
second horn preserves a measure of independence in the lower
range while the first horn merrily skips up to e'''—concert b'',
only a semitone lower than Stamitz's concert c'' in Example 139.
(Example 142) Among the many Pokorny symphonies falsely
ascribed to other composers, there are five to which Bernasconi's

name has been attached. In the second of these, a *Symphony in D*, the melody in the first section of the Trio is of a more angular type, almost like a yodel. (Example 143) Note with what skill the melody has been constructed: the melody of the first two bars is answered, but without the triplet, in the next two

Ex. 142

Horns in G

bars, and the rhythmic figure of a quarter followed by a half becomes two eighths plus a half at the beginning of the second section. Note also, in the second section, how the paired eighths in the third bar are answered unsymmetrically in the fifth bar, and then how the same high note, c''', in the sixth bar gains interest by syncopation. In this Trio the peak note is only d''' and a less formidable technique is required, but it is full of sparkling, imaginative melody of which only a master could be capable.

At the Thurn and Taxis Library there are two *Symphonies in D* to which Sammartini's name is attached. One of them (T.&T.4) is identical with Pokorny's *Symphony No. 45*, and the other (T.&T.3) is undoubtedly also by Pokorny. Certainly the Trio in the latter symphony is in the Regensburg master's most genial

Ex. 143

Horns in D

style. (Example 144) Here the first horn plays sustained, lyric melody in the *clarino* range—quite different from Sammartini's pedestrian writing for horns. But it is the second horn part that points unmistakably to Pokorny, for it is almost wholly in triplet eighths, with two groups of descending sixteenths to clinch the matter.

A final example of Pokorny's Trio melody is taken from a *Symphony in E flat* (T.&T.92), by which Monn was honored since his name was substituted for that of the rightful composer. (Example 145) Again Pokorny has paid great attention to

rhythm and contour in his horn melody: the opening motive in the first horn (it is identical with that of Example 144) is freely restated a fifth higher in the second phrase of the first section, and then this restatement recurs twice more, with slight variants, in the balancing half of the second section. Counting repetitions, the first hornist had to reach g''' (concert bb'') by skip six times!

The second horn, forced to be on his guard constantly because of the leaps and changing range, also is given three of Pokorny's amusing little descending fanfares.

v. Finale. *La Chasse*

In the Finale of the eighteenth-century symphony, the function of the brass was, to an extent, dependent upon the form of the movement. Like the first movement, the Finale might be in Sonata-Allegro form, and the brass would then add festive weight, as at the unforgettable beginning of the C major Finale of Beethoven's *Fifth Symphony*, where the horns double the pompous trumpets in the lower octave. (Example 146)

Ex. 146.

ff Trumpets and Horns in C

When the Finale was in variation form, the brass would probably shine in certain variations only. Typical variation treatment occurs in the Andante con Variazioni of a Krommer *Parthia in E flat* (T.&T.13/1), where the horns are brilliant in the third of six sections. Again, in the Andante con Variazioni of Haydn's *Octet in F*, the horn plays an expressive melody in the third variation. However, these two Andantes were not Finales. The solo horn dominates throughout the Minuetto cantabile con Variationi, the last movement of Punto's *Eleventh Horn Concerto* in E, and plays the unadorned melody only in the Coda. (See Example 108.)

The most common form for the Finale, the rondo, presented the brass an invitation to put its best foot forward in the recurring rondo theme. It is no accident that almost all of Rosetti's and Punto's horn concertos end with a Rondeau, the latter's just mentioned *Eleventh Concerto* being an exception. The association of horns with rondo form frequently resulted in a *chasse*-like movement, to be discussed at the end of this section. A very different type of rondo theme occurs in the Andante of Pokorny's *Serenade in D*, where the solo horn plays with the charm of Haydn. (See Example 129.)

The rondo Finale was seldom as serious as a movement in Sonata-Allegro form. But it seems as impressive as a Bach fugue compared to the Presto Finale in $\frac{3}{8}$ meter. The Finale in $\frac{3}{8}$ meter was the least desirable part of the inheritance taken over by the concert symphony from the Italian overture. With a beat so fast that only occasionally did a pair of sixteenths occur, but with such strong accents that the ear did not tend to group bars to form larger units of $\frac{6}{8}$ or $\frac{12}{8}$, the Italianate Finale was in general as trivial as could be imagined. Within the key the harmony was almost wholly tonic and dominant, and brief excursions to the dominant key were often the extent of the modulations.

A typical Italian Finale can be found in the overture to Piccini's opera, *La Buona Figliuola*, which is cast in an amorphous form. (A piano reduction of Piccinni's overture is printed in Einstein's *Beispielsammlung zur Musikgeschichte*, p. 69.) With such harmonic barrenness, it was natural for the brass to be playing most of the time, and this was actually the case. The Finale of a Graun *Symphony in F* is even in simple binary form, and it is notable only for the pedal notes for the second horn. (Example 147)

Ex. 147

Horns in F

Among the earlier composers of symphonic music, Zach's *Flute Concerto in G* has a good example of the $\frac{3}{8}$ Finale. Here the horns (called "clarinetti obligatti" in the score) play a naive tune which resembles the Civil War song, *Tenting Tonight*. (Example 148) In the Thurn and Taxis Library there are a dozen

Ex. 148

Horns in G

symphonies (only four with brass) by Zach's slightly younger contemporary, Jommelli. In every one of these symphonies the Finale is in $\frac{3}{8}$, and is almost wholly devoid of musical ideas.

The $\frac{3}{8}$ Finale was especially favored at the Palatinate and

Thurn-and-Taxis courts, being written at Mannheim by Johann Stamitz, Christian Cannabich, and Filtz, and at Regensburg by Pokorny, Donninger, and Schacht. Pokorny could make something substantial, even from the Italianate Finale, for in the Finale Presto of one of his forty symphonies in D (it is dated, "Hocheraltheim [sic], June 25, 1755") there is a horn duet twenty-one bars in length. (Example 149) In this passage there is a fine

Ex. 149

Horns in D

melodic flow for the first horn, rising to an effective climax on c'''; the second horn genially abets the situation with varied figures of arpeggios, thirds with the melody, and detached notes. (By the way, Righini is the ghost whose name appears with this Pokorny symphony, T.&T.32.)

In two other Pokorny symphonies in D major at Regensburg (T.&T.22, 59), the time signature of the last movement was originally $\frac{3}{8}$; but was later changed to $\frac{6}{8}$, with alternate barlines scratched out. Both symphonies were originally for flutes, horns, and strings, and it is interesting that the trumpet parts, which were added later, were in $\frac{6}{8}$. (The first of these symphonies is dated "Hohenaltheim, May 2, 1761.") Similarly, an *E flat Symphony* by Johann Stamitz (DTB Es 1, T.&T.14) for oboes, horns, and strings has a Prestissimo fourth movement in which all of the instruments are notated in $\frac{3}{8}$ save for the violins, which are given greater dignity through a $\frac{6}{8}$ barring.

The above preference for a $\frac{6}{8}$ over the $\frac{3}{8}$ signature is probably a reflection of the colorful *chasse* Finale, found so often in the eighteenth-century symphony and concerto. Haydn's *Symphony No. 73* in D contains such a Finale; certain symphonies and concertos by Mozart and Beethoven have *chasse* intimations (See

Example 154.); and those stalwart penners of horn concertos, Punto and Rosetti, have added their contributions to the genre. In fact, so important was the *chasse* in the music of this period that it will be advisable to trace its history in detail.

For the early history of hunting music I owe much to Alexander L. Ringer's fascinating Columbia dissertation, *The Chasse*, where we are informed about the French *chace* and the Italian *caccia* in the fourteenth-century Ars Nova; Jannequin's *La Chasse* of 1528 and the anonymous "Wohlauf" in Forster's lieder collection of 1540. The English had such virginal pieces as *The Hunt's Up, The Hunting Galliard, The King's Hunt*. There are several delightful little hunting songs in Ravenscroft's collection of 1614 entitled *Brief Discourse . . . Concerning the Pleasure of Five Usual Recreations*—the recreations being hunting, hawking, dancing, drinking, and enamouring.

The earliest French hunting calls were mere rhythmic shouts ("huées") similar to the dots and dashes of Morse code. They were superseded by the "cornures," which carried farther than the human voice, but still were without significant melodic variation. After the simple horn was replaced by the circular "trompe" during the seventeenth century, the stage was set for the appearance of the first classical *sonneries* during the reign of Louis XIV. (Jacques Du Fouilloux quotes the verses, "Lorsque les fanfares parurent, Les cornures en moururent.")

The earliest of these *sonneries* were the seven composed by Philidor the Elder and contained in a Versailles manuscript dated 1705. Only one of Philidor's calls, No. 6, "La retraite," was in the conventional $\frac{6}{8}$ meter; it was modified by Dampierre for "La retraite prise." (See Example 150 n.) The best-known of Philidor's calls was No. 7, "La sourcillade," named in honor of the king's "lieutenant de la vénerie en 1703." Originally in duple meter, it became Dampierre's "La vue." (See Example 150(e).) But before this time it had appeared in true hunting rhythm in Morin's *divertissement* for voices and instruments, *La Chasse du Cerf*, 1708. Except for the introductory "Le Reveil" for horn or oboe (See Example 26.), Morin's substantial work was entirely in $\frac{6}{8}$ or $\frac{3}{8}$.

The most honored name in the history of the classic hunting calls is that of Marquis Marc Antoine de Dampierre, 1676-1756. His earliest calls were composed at the beginning of the reign

Ex. 150 (a)

French Hunting Calls for Horns

(b)

(c)

(d)

Fine

D. C.

(e)

(f)

Fine

D. C.

(g)

(h)

1. 2.

(i)

Fine

D. C.

D. C.

of Louis XV. Six of his calls which date from 1723 or later are included among the examples shown below; these are "Debuché," "Volcelet," "Vue," "Hallali," "Retraite prise," and "Retour de la Chasse." (Examples 150 (h), (f), (e), (m), (n), and (o)) The complete collection of Dampierre's twenty-nine calls was published posthumously in 1778.

From the musical point of view the most important group of *sonneries* are those dealing with the progress of the hunt ("fanfares de circonstances"), from the unleashing of the dogs until they are shut up again in their kennels. A second group of calls ("fanfares des animaux") referred to the type and age of the quarry, such as "Le Sanglier" (the Gamecock) and "Le Daguet" (Stag in its second year). These were important in the hunt itself, but lacked appeal to composers. An entire hunt could be portrayed musically by incorporating the "fanfares de circonstances" in the proper order. Our examples are taken exclusively from this group. (The calls and their description have been taken from several sources, the most trustworthy of which seems to be the *Nouveau Larousse Illustré*. However, it gives the calls for one horn only, and the two-horn version is followed in the musical compositions using the calls.)

"Quête" is a fanfare sounded after the dogs have been unleashed; it encourages them to find a trace of the stag. (Example 150 (a)) The fanfare, "Premier Ton des Chiens," (b) is also used to encourage the dogs, as is "Autre Ton suivant la Chasse." (c) "Lancé" warns the hunters to be on guard, since the stag is afoot. (d) The first sight of the quarry's entire body is marked by "Vue," (e) and here comes the shout of "Tayaut" (Tallyho). But if only the stag's foot is visible, one shouts "Volcelet" (an abbreviation for "Vois-le, ce l'est") and the shout gives its name to the call. (f) "Fort Vue" indicates a glimpse of the stag in a heavily wooded district. (g) "Débuché" means that he has taken to the open country. (h) "Bat-l'eau" ("à l'eau") is sounded when the stag has plunged into the water to evade the dogs (i), and "Sortie de l'eau" when he has returned to dry land. (j) When the stag has eluded the dogs, one shouts to them "Derrière, derrière" and sounds the "Hourvari." (k) The hunt is resumed with "Relancé," the first two bars of which serve for the *sonnerie* "Retour" (l) ("Retour" indicates that the stag has abruptly shifted his direction.) The "Hallali" represents the high point of the hunt, when the dogs have set upon the stag—the first part when the animal is still standing ("debout"), the second part for the actual death ("par terre"). (m) Then "Retraite prise" calls off the dogs (n), and "Retour de la Chasse" is the signal for the return home. (o) Finally, "Curée" is to summon the dogs to their repast, either on the stag's entrails ("chaude") or on its blood ("froide"). (p)

As a rule, an orchestral *chasse* movement would use only one of the French calls. Near the beginning of the *chasse* Finale of Haydn's *Symphony No. 73* in D, 1780, the horns play *Vue* (Philidor's *Sourcillade* Example 150 (e)), and this strain returns identically near the end of the movement. The slow movement of Lang's *Concerto da Caccia* in D, an Andantino in $\frac{3}{8}$, is based on the *Bat-l'eau*, the escape by water (i), and its Finale is likewise based on only one *sonnerie*, the *Retraite prise* (n). In Gossec's *Sinfonia la Caccia* in D, 1774, the Allegretto quasi Allegro in D minor (the closest approach to a slow movement in this work) has a Trio in F in which the horns sound the *Bat-l'eau*, and the Finale has a full-fledged *Hallali* (m).

One hunting call which composers have found useful does not belong properly in the list of the French *sonneries*, for it is not concerned with the progress of the hunt. This is the popular French song, "Pour aller à la chasse," the so-called *Hubertus Aria*, reputedly relished by Count Sporck, who introduced the French *parforce* horn to Bohemia. (Example 151) Named for

Ex. 151

Hubertus Melody for Horns

the patron saint of hunting, the tune was played principally on his day, November 3. Ringer (op. cit., p. 208) has given something of the history of the tune, including its resemblance to the Dutch national anthem, *Wilhelmus*. Since Kappey (*Military Music*, p. 49) has presented a version of the *Wilhelmus* melody dated 1568, as well as a German trumpet arrangement of it dated 1603, any borrowing would seem to have been from the French side.

Sebastian Bach has incorporated *St. Hubert's Tune* in the *Peasant Cantata*, as the melody of the bass aria in G, "Es nehme zehn tausend Ducaten." For no better reason than the hunting associations of this tune, Bach has added obbligato horns to the accompaniment. An allusion to the *Hubertus* melody is contained also in Leopold Mozart's *Sinfonia da Caccia*, composed in 1756, the year of Wolfgang's birth. (According to Ringer, the tune is said to have been a bedtime favorite of the infant Wolfgang.) The work is written for two horns in G, two horns in D, and strings. The first movement begins with the G horns sounding a call that resembles the latter part of the *Bat-l'eau*. Later, as part of the second subject, the D horns develop a dotted-note motive that is plainly derived from the *Hubertus* tune. The exposition and the reprise end with the simple fanfares shown in Example 124.

Modifications of the hunting calls are the rule rather than the exception when they have been employed in art music. Ringer (his Example 63) has shown a passage from a *Quintet* by Boccherini in which the first cello, imitated by the second cello, plays a variant of the beginning of *Relancé* (Example 150 (1)). A similar motive is shown from Karl Stamitz' *Concerto for Viola d'Amore in D*, where double stops are a reasonably satisfactory substitute for a pair of horns. (Example 152) But here the phrase

Ex. 152

Viola d'Amore

ends with a motive that might have been derived from the half cadence of any one of half a dozen of the tunes shown in Example 150. Ringer compares this with a strikingly similar passage in duple meter for solo horn in a symphony by Hoffmeister.

(Ringer's Example 67) In Beethoven's *Rondo for Piano and Orchestra* in B flat there is a somewhat similar horn passage, concealed by chromatic appoggiaturas in the other instruments.

From the Finale of the same Hoffmeister symphony just discussed, Ringer has quoted another hunting call, which begins like the *Bat-l'eau,* followed by the ascending scale from *Sortie de l'eau* or *Débuché.* (Ringer's Example 68) In the Allegro of Karl Stamitz' *Sinfonia la Caccia* in D (DTB D 10) the call begins with the repeated g' of *Quête* and continues with what is essentially *Retraite prise.* In Croes' *Symphony in D* (T.&T.24) there is a more lengthy call, which begins with the descending scale from *Relancé;* its second strain is a faithful version of the corresponding half of *Hallali*—"l'hallali par terre."

It must be admitted that in many *chasse*-like movements the connection with the French *sonneries* is very tenuous. The $\frac{6}{8}$ meter is a prime requisite, of course, as well as a melody restricted to six notes and accompanied in horn style. So, although the opening bars of Mendelssohn's *Song Without Words in A*, Opus 19, No. 3, do not resemble any of the calls in Example 150, they convey the atmosphere of the hunt. (Example 153) Although

Ex. 153

Piano

Mendelssohn himself did not label his piece *Jägerlied,* it comes as close to the true genre as many of the works or movements for violin and piano or for piano alone which Ringer has listed with such titles as "La Chasse," "La Caccia," or "Die Jagd."

If, in addition to the hunting meter and the hunting melody, actual horns are playing, the illusion is complete, no matter whether the tunes are based on *sonneries* of the *chasse royale* or not. The beautiful principal themes of the Finales of Mozart's *First* and *Second Horn Concertos* in D and E flat, respectively, are idealized *sonneries.* Example 154 gives an excerpt from the former concerto. (The rondo theme of Punto's *Sixth Horn Concerto* in E flat bears a strong resemblance to the Mozart

Ex. 154

Horn in D

theme in the same key.) Note also the hunting themes in the Allegretto of Beethoven's *Sixth Symphony* and the Vivace of his *Seventh Symphony*.

Often one suspects that a particular hunting passage has been influenced by some other type of music. In Example 152 from the Stamitz *Viola d'Amore Concerto* both the final and the half cadence have repeated notes, as does its counterpart in duple meter from the Hoffmeister symphony. Two early symphonies by Mozart, *Symphony No. 16* in C and *No. 17* in G have *chasse* Finales in which the horns similarly end a phrase with repeated notes. But cadential repeated notes are not found at all in the French *sonneries*, which may use instead a changing-note figure for the half cadence, as in Examples 150 (d), (h), (i), (m), (n), and (o).

On the other hand, repeated notes are not uncharacteristic of cadences of the gigue—or of its country cousin, the jig, as in *The Irish Washerwoman*. However, a gigue is more often in $\frac{12}{8}$ than in $\frac{6}{8}$ and only very rarely is a *chasse* movement in the former meter, the Leopold Mozart symphony illustrated in Example 124 being an exception. The $\frac{12}{8}$ meter is also found for a jiggy horn passage in movements which Handel has thriftily used in his *Organ Concerto in F* and the *Concerto for Two Choirs*, as well as in the ritornello of the alto aria, "Io seguo sol fiero," in his opera, *Partenope*. It is beyond the scope of the present study to consider any possible connection between the artistically treated *sonneries* and dances like the gigue. I suggest this as a topic for future research.

To conclude this chapter, I should like to refer to several works in which the *sonneries* were employed extensively and also retained in a recognizable form. Such a use of the French hunting calls was made in the *Concerto da Caccia* in D by Johann Georg Lang (1724-post 1794). This work, in the Thurn and Taxis Library, is ostensibly a harpsichord concerto, but is much more in the style of a concertante symphony, with important horn parts. The cembalist also played a continuo part and conducted the orchestra, for not only were there continuous cues for him, but the names of the calls were attached to his part when these were played by horns or other instruments.

The first movement of Lang's *Concerto* tells the complete story of a successful hunt, using in order the classic calls: "Quête" (a), "Lancé" (d), "Vue" (e), "Tons pour les Chiens" ("Autre Ton . . .") (c), "Hourvari" (k), "Relancé" (l), "Volcelet" (f), "Débuché" (h), and "Hallali" (m). Reference has already been made to the fact that Lang's Andante and Finale were based on a single *sonnerie* each. The Finale is an especially weak movement; but the first movement, at least, will repay careful study by anyone interested in the part played in art music by the hunting calls.

In addition to the telescoped pair of calls shown in Example 152, Karl Stamitz, in the Rondo Finale of his *Concerto for Viola d'Amore*, has assigned to the solo instrument the *Hallali, Bat-l'eau* and *Débuché*. Although the first movement of Stamitz' *Sinfonia la Caccia* contains the previously mentioned synthetic call (*Quête* plus *Retraite prise*), the Allegro più Moderato movement has a clear *Bat-l'eau*, and the Presto has an excellent *Hallali*, as well as a reasonably faithful *Vue*. Gossec's *Sinfonia da Caccia* in D is another work in which the presentation of the hunting calls took precedence over musical development. In the Tempo di Caccia movement his horns play free versions of *Quête* and *Volcelet*, as well as a rather strict *Sortie de l'eau*. Later movements contain the *Bat-l'eau* and a full-fledged *Hallali*, the best-known of all the calls.

One of the most famous orchestral compositions featuring the French *sonneries* is *La Chasse du Jeune Henri*, the overture to Méhul's opera, *Le Jeune Henri*, 1795. It has four horns in D and two horns in A. Méhul is a model of restraint in his treatment of the horn calls, reserving them for effective and climactic moments. The opening Andante, portraying the beauties of the morning, has only fanfaring calls. In the *chasse* proper there is an ingratiating call not included in Example 150; it is played softly by the A horns and repeated by the tutti with more sophisticated harmony. (Example 155 (a)) Later, a motive from the *Bat-l'eau* is developed, and the joyful *Hallali* enters toward the end, repeated with sufficiently complex harmonies that they should be shown. (Example 155 (b)) Ordinarily the composers made no attempt to improve upon the simple tonic and dominant harmony of the calls.

The outstanding specimen of hunting music is the chorus, "Hört, das laute Getön," in the Autumn section of Haydn's

Seasons. His hunt begins in D with *Quête*. Ringer identifies a following *sonnerie* as *Lancé*; it seems, if anything, to be a variant of *Relancé*. (Example 156 (a)) *Débuché* comes next. The signal for the stag's temporary escape is *Volcelet*, commencing

with its middle part. At this point Haydn increases the tension by raising the general pitch a semitone to E flat, where it remains until the end of the chorus. The first call in the new key is *Retour*. Ringer calls the next call *Fort Vue*; it shows only slight resemblance to the single example of this call which I have found listed elsewhere. (Example 156 (b)) The *Hallali* occurs with unchallenged authority, with the voices twice repeating its phrase. Finally there is the *Retour de la Chasse*, which Ringer has confused with the *Retraite prise*—the calls are alike only in their cadences.

I have a special attachment to Haydn's chorus, having heard it at the Musikverein in Vienna in 1954, on a very warm Whittuesday. When the four hornists turned up the bells of their instruments and intoned in unison the summons to the hunt, something like an electric shock went through the audience. By the time the triumphant *Hallali* rang out from instruments and voices, one almost rose from one's seat. This one superb chorus is perhaps sufficient justification for all the groping efforts to capture the essence of the chase that were made before Haydn's masterpiece.

CHAPTER IV

Pitch

i. High Trumpets and Horns

Mersenne in the *Harmonie Universelle* had given c''' as the top note of the trumpet, and this note was reached in many of the little pieces in Fantini's collection two years later. There was even a d''' in Fantini's "Seconda ricercate detta l'Acciaioli," a brilliant miniature with well-varied rhythms. (Example 157) Since Fantini

Ex. 157

Trumpet in C or D

indicated in the title of his book that its contents were intended not only for the ordinary military trumpet in C but also for the muted trumpet in D, his d''' would represent e''' in concert pitch.

In general, however, the solo trumpet parts of the seventeenth and eighteenth centuries, with all their sparkling arpeggios and runs, did not go extremely high. The peak would often be g'' or a'', and Mersenne's c''' was rarely exceeded. In half a dozen examples already shown in this book the trumpet has gone above c''', the sixteenth partial. The note d''' on the C trumpet was touched lightly in a florid, imitative passage in Buxtehude's *Alleluia* (Example 36) and in a very similar passage in Bach's *Cantata 31*. (Example 50)

In a score of works Sebastian Bach wrote higher than c''' for trumpet. In his fugue-cantata, "Nun ist das Heil und die Kraft," (*Cantata No. 50*), the first trumpet in D takes up the fugue subject as a fifth voice, and, accompanied homophonically by the other two trumpets, reaches a quarter-note d'''. When the trumpet is later assigned the subject, it is in the form of the answer and ascends only to c''', preceded by several bb''. (Examples 158

Ex. 158 (a)

Trumpets in D

(b)

(a) and (b)) This same high note has been shown in Examples 53 and 93, in polyphonic passages for a pair of trumpets in two different *Symphonies in D* by Richter, and also was present in a symphony by Anton Eberl, dated 1783.

Concert e''' might also be obtained as the twentieth harmonic on a C trumpet, as in the duet between trumpet and soprano voice in Caldara's *Iphigenia in Aulis*. (Example 39) In the concluding chorale of Bach's *Cantata 31*, from which Example 50 had been taken, the first trumpet, supported by the first violins, has a high obbligato part which reaches e'''. Since such a rhythmically independent part above a chorale melody is different from any of the usages shown in Examples 61 through 72, Example 159 presents the melody and the obbligato for the entire chorale. (In a way this example is the counterpart of Example 63, in which the second horn had an independent part below the melody.) Still another example of e''' on the C trumpet deserves special mention: in the fifth act of Caldara's opera, *I due dittatori*, the first trumpet plays a passage of ascending quarter notes orna-

mented by turns, with its climax on d'''; the second trumpet
then repeats this passage exactly. Later, by way of eight trilled
half notes, the first trumpet ascends to e''', and the second trumpet again repeats the passage, note for note! This e''' would seem
to be the high water mark for second trumpet in the eighteenth
century. (Example 160)

Ex. 159

Trumpet I and Violin I; Soprano, Oboes I and II, Violin II

In the *Second Brandenburg Concerto* Bach has written many
c''' for the solo trumpet in F—unforgettably in the fugue subject
of the Finale. (See Example 44 (b).) In the first movement of this
work there is a D-minor arpeggio for the trumpet, with leaps
from a'' to d''' and back again. This high note, concert g''', occurs with greater melodic significance on the F trumpet in the
excerpt from Telemann's *Violin Concerto* which was shown in
Example 4. The same pitch was reached the hard way (by what
a mountain climber or military tactician would call a frontal as-

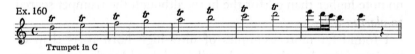

Ex. 160

Trumpet in C

sault) in Caldara's *I due dittatori*, where the fantastically difficult
trumpet part, understandably, was provided with an *ossia*. (See
Example 193.)

As horns became more firmly established in the symphony
orchestra, they gradually usurped the *clarino* range, together
with the *clarino* function. In two very early *Symphonies in D*
by Richter, the first being dated 1741 (See Examples 53 and 93.),
the trumpets play polyphonically and more interestingly than the

horns; in both symphonies the first trumpet reaches d''', the
first horn, c'''. In later decades, even if trumpet and horn reached
the same written high note, the horns would be assigned the more
melodic part. But more commonly the first trumpet was not
asked to play as high as c''' in the symphonies, even when the
first horn was. For example, in the *D major Symphony* by
Johann Stamitz illustrated in Example 98 the horn reaches c''',
but the trumpet, only g''. In *Symphonies in D* by Pallavicini
(T.&T.2) and Pokorny (T.&T.46; he was misnamed Princess
Maria Theresia of Thurn and Taxis, Countess of Ahlefeldt) the
horn again played c''', but the trumpet had to be content with e''.

   Although most of the extremely high notes for horns discussed
later in this section occurred in symphonies without trumpets,
there was a Wranitzky *Symphony in D* in which the first horn
reached e''' (See Example 92.), whereas the trumpet had a humdrum g'' for his top note. Even in the decadent period at the end
of the century, when the horn was not required to play above g''
or a'', composers would make a distinction between horn and
trumpet, as in Danzi's *Grande Sinfonie* in B flat, where the horn
plays g'', the trumpet e'', or in a *Symphony in C* by Wenzel
Müller (T.&T.1, 1790), where the horn plays a'' and the
trumpet, e''. There are also eighteen little *Harmoniestücke*
(T.&T. Inc. IV(a) 23) for two horns and a trumpet, in the
Thurn and Taxis Library, and in these the first horn may go to
g'', but the trumpet only to c''. It should be mentioned, as an
extraordinary exception for the time when it was written (1783),
that the autograph score of a *Symphony in D* by Eberl contained
no note higher than g'' for the horn, although the trumpet soared
to *clarino* d'''.

   I found far more examples of ultra-high horn parts than of
trumpet parts, but these are heavily weighted by the large number of symphonies examined at the Thurn and Taxis Library,
especially those by the prolific Pokorny. From the present evidence, it seems likely that when *clarino* players transferred their
astounding talents from trumpet to horn, they were able to produce approximately the same range of high notes.

   With both horns and trumpets, "high" may be considered in
two ways, either as the written note, representing a certain harmonic, or as the absolute pitch of the tone produced. It would

seem reasonable that the lower the fundamental pitch of the instrument, the higher the harmonics that could be produced on it, but that in absolute pitch the highest notes would be produced on instruments which had the highest fundamental pitch. This is illustrated in the rule-of-thumb by which one determines whether a movement in B flat was to be played on the *B alto* or the *B basso* horns, when the composer himself had not specified which to use. Very often, a movement in B flat would have the written c''' as the top note for the first horn, in which case the *B basso* was intended; if g'' was the highest note, the horn would probably be the *B alto*. But in absolute pitch these two extreme notes are bb' and f'' respectively—that is, the higher note in absolute pitch is produced on the higher-pitched horn.

This common result on the B-flat horns agrees with the rough general rule that the absolute pitch rises half as fast as the fundamental of the horn—the highest note on an E horn might be expected to be a tone higher in absolute pitch than that of a C horn, and likewise that of a G horn over that of an E-flat horn. As luck would have it, this rule is illustrated precisely with the highest notes found on horns in these four keys.

The written note c''' was encountered so frequently in music of the eighteenth century that we shall consider as high only a note that is at least d'''. Among the works examined in the present study, ninety-four contained such notes, distributed as follows: Bb horn, 2; C horn, 12; D horn, 40; Eb horn, 22; E horn, 4; F horn, 9; G horn, 5. It will be observed that almost half of the high notes were found on the D horn. To a large extent this reflects the tremendous popularity of this key in the earliest stage of the symphony, D being of course the favorite *clarino* key. The horn in E flat had greater beauty of tone and was used overwhelmingly in chamber music, and so it is no surprise that there should have been many instances of its use—in fact it was better represented on the very highest notes than the D horn was. Both C and E were among the less popular keys for the horn, and, although F and G were common enough keys, they were so high in pitch that the written c''' was seldom exceeded.

The examples are arranged according to the concert pitch of the highest note, from c'' to c''', some of these notes being capable of being produced in four or five different ways. Since

composers did not ordinarily write the extremely high notes
except when they had something interesting to say, most of the
examples will have their principal listing elsewhere in this book,
especially as illustrations of minuet melody or as the combination
of two horns in contrasted style.

The lowest of the "high" notes, c″, occurred as d‴ on a horn
in B♭ *basso*, in a dance-like passage in Rameau's motet, "Diligam
te, Domine." (Example 110) A half-note e‴ played on a horn
in B♭ *basso* in the fugal Finale of a Pokorny symphony gave the
concert pitch d″. (Example 54) The concert d″ as written d‴
on a C horn was present in seven works, including two Pokorny
symphonies. In the one symphony (T.&T.2) the d‴ was touched
lightly twice in an Andante movement, with the second horn
playing smooth triplets like those in Example 59. But in the other
Symphony in C (T.&T.1), near the end of the Allegro, the first
horn plays the d‴ for an entire bar, with the second horn a sixth
below. (Example 161)

Ex. 161

Horns in C

Concert e″ will be represented either as d‴ on the D horn or
as e‴ on the C horn. The former note was extremely common,
twenty-six instances having been located. It was found in three
minuets by Pokorny (Examples 143, 144 and 149), each in a
symphony which had also been ascribed to another composer. An
even more dramatic appearance of this note is in the first movement of Haydn's *First Horn Concerto* in D. In Example 123 a
quarter-note d‴ was shown, approached by step, in the Adagio
of this concerto. But in the Allegro the d‴ is the culminating
note of a dominant arpeggio, and is sustained for three beats.
(Example 162) One further example of d‴ on the D horn is
wholly uninteresting, save for the fact that in this unison passage
in a Huber *Symphony in D* is the only found instance of a second
horn playing the eighteenth harmonic. (Example 163)

As for the written e‴ on the C horn, only three examples were
located, one of which, however, from the Adagio of a Haymann
Oboe Concerto in C, is a remarkable, florid duet for trumpet and

horn in sixths, the horn part, of course, being written a third higher than the trumpet but sounding a sixth below it. (Example 164)

Concert f″ may be either written d‴ on the horn in E flat or f‴ on the horn in C. Three illustrations have been shown of the

Ex. 162

Horn in D

former note: barely touched in a passage in a Pokorny symphony (Example 116), and as the culminating note of a twelve-note scale starting on g′, both in a Rosetti *Horn Concerto* (Example 104) and the Beethoven *Sextet.* (Example 119) For the f‴ on the C horn we turn to the same *Oboe Concerto* by Haymann from which Example 164 was taken. In fact, only a dozen bars

Ex. 163

Unison Horns in D

later than the duet for trumpet and horn, the first horn trills blithely up to e‴ and follows it with the f‴. (Example 165)

There are two feasible ways for f♯″ to occur as a top note for horn, either as d″ on the E horn or as e‴ on the D horn. Only the second of these notes was found, with the largest incidence of any of the superacute notes except d‴ on the D horn, —ten compared with twenty-six. The earliest illustration shown

Ex. 164

Trumpet in C

Horn in C

was from Zelenka's *Minuet in D*, the first strain of which was given in Example 138. Its melodic style is familiar enough; the wonder is that it was not written several decades later than it was. From Regensburg came a typical Pokorny duet, with arpeggios in the second horn (Example 117), and the antiphonal treatment by Schacht of two pairs of horns. (Example 60) Haydn, in a *clarino*-like passage in a *Sinfonie Concertante*, contributed five e′″ (Example 47), and Wranitzky reached this note by way of a flourish. (Example 92)

Of the four possible ways to produce g″ (d′″ on the F horn, e′″ on the E♭ horn, f′″ on the D horn, and g′″ on the C horn),

Ex. 165

Horn in C

all were represented in our examples, although the g′″ was not the top note on the C horn. The d′″ on the F horn was illustrated from Bach's *Hercules* (Example 52) and the Pokorny *Double Concerto* (Example 59), in both of which illustrations the horns converse amiably together. (It was with such precedents that I wrote a d′″ in Example 69, to show how a difficult chorale might have been treated.) The e′″ on the E♭ horn occurred in a passage of florid thirds written by Touchemolin. (Example 46) The highest harmonic found on the D horn was f′″, the twenty-second harmonic. Of four instances, two were by Pokorny, not included in our examples (T.&T.31, 161); the other two came from symphonies by Leopold Mozart, in one of which (Example 35) the horn played polyphonically with the violins, while in the other it soared in the best *clarino* manner. (Example 91)

The semitone above g″ might be either g♯″ or a♭″. As the former note it would be e′″ on the E horn, and this note is prominent in the Schacht *Double Concerto* (Example 120), although it is not the climactic note of the passage. The a♭″ would be played as f′″ on the horn in E flat, of which eight or nine instances were found. Pokorny has provided two sparkling illustrations in Examples 118 and 58, the former generating excitement by the gradual rise of the melody and the widespread triplets in the second horn, the latter being more conventionally polyphonic in a passage beginning in A minor.

Another expressive use of f′″ on the E♭ horn to produce concert a♭″ occurs in the Adagio of Haydn's *Symphony No. 51* in B flat. Here the first horn in E flat has an eight-bar solo. There is a dramatic contrast between the simple arc of the antecedent phrase and the soaring line of the consequent phrase, followed by a bold downward leap of a tenth. (Example 166)

Potentially, a″ might have been produced in any one of six ways: d‴ on the G horn; e‴ on the F horn; f‴ on the E horn; f#″ on the E♭ horn; g‴ on the D horn; and a‴ on the C horn.

Ex. 166

Horn in E♭

The d‴ on the G horn was shown in Example 72, a canonic passage in Bach's *Cantata 128*. (It also occurs in the Sinfonia to his *Cantata 174*, which turns out to be the first movement of the *Third Brandenburg Concerto*, with added horns and oboes.) Again, there are two whole bars of d‴ in the Allegro con spiritoso of a *Symphony in G* (T.&T.13) by Christian Canna-bich—a typically unimaginative treatment that strongly suggests the *clarino* style, with its rhythmically repeated notes and open fourths. (Example 167) Note that the entire passage could be

Ex. 167

Horns in G

played with open notes an octave lower; so that trumpets in G, had any been available, could have caused the passage to sound at the same concert pitch as the horns, but with much less trouble.

We are by no means through with the possibilities of produc-ing a″ on the horn. In the Finale (Presto assai) of the *Double Concerto* from which Example 59 was taken, representing con-cert g″, Pokorny's first horn in F reaches e‴, or concert a″. (Example 168) If the master's touch is not quite so evident in

Ex. 168

Horns in F

this example, it is present in all of its glory in Example 169. Here in the Allegro assai of a Pokorny *Symphony in E* (T.&T.66; Agrell is the false name this time), the first horn has bold leaps in the superacute region, culminating on f'''; meanwhile the second horn has two bars of the telltale arpeggio triplets.

A separate paragraph is needed for the a''' for C horn from a minuet by Veichtner, given in Example 141. Perhaps it is not the best minuet melody written for horn; but it is a good melody, and has the distinction of being just a little higher than anyone else dared to write. Did Veichtner have a particular player in

Ex. 169

Horns in E

mind? The fact that this symphony was published is an indication that there must have been a quorum of players in Europe whose technique was equal to its difficulties.

As a peak note, bb'' always appeared as g''' on the horn in E flat. (If the horns in the second Trio of Haydn's *Symphony No. 51* were in Bb *alto*, the highest written note, c''', also sounds bb''. And see the Rosetti Example 187.) In Example 145 this note had been reached by skip three times in a Pokorny minuet. (Somewhat less spectacular was its appearance in a dominant arpeggio, in the Allegro assai of a Pokorny *Symphony in E flat* (T.&T. 88) from which no illustrations have been culled. There is a half-note f''' in the following bar.) A minuet by Johann Stamitz (Example 140) showed the g''' attained by step and quitted by leap. In the Romance Andantino of a *Parthia in E flat*, allegedly by Buschmann, the g''' also comes at the end of a scale. The vigorous octave arpeggios at the beginning of this passage suggest that the real composer may have been Stamitz, for no other composer of the century wrote horn octaves with such thrilling mastery. (Example 170)

With b'' we reach a rarefied atmosphere indeed. As e''' on the G horn it has been cited in the Minuet Trio of a Pokorny symphony. (Example 142) As the more difficult g''' on the E horn,

Ex. 170

Horns in Eb

an extremely brilliant example of its use has been presented in a concerto for two horns by Schacht, in which the climax is pure arpeggio melody. (Example 120) Reicha, in the Allegro of a *Concerto Concertante for Two Horns in E* Op. 5, reached the g''' via a fast G-major scale, possibly a glissando, similar to the scale in Example 170. It is interesting to observe that both Schacht and Reicha used stopped notes very freely in other parts of these two concertos, a practice that in general was accompanied by a decline in the *clarino* treatment of the horn.

Finally we come to the c''', which is probably not a *ne plus ultra*, an Everest summit, but more likely just an obvious goal, like the four-minute mile. Only one instance of this note was found, as f''' on the G horn, in a Stamitz minuet. (Example 139) It is fitting that this most skilled composer for horns should have penned the note that so far as is known at present is the highest in absolute pitch ever to have been written for horn during the eighteenth century. It was probably, however, no more difficult to produce this note than concert b'' on the E horn, bb'' on the Eb horn, or a'' on the C horn—and Stamitz was responsible for several of these notes also!

Two conclusions may rather easily be drawn from our study of high horn notes. In the first place, extremely good *primo* players had to be available, or else there would have been no point at all in writing these notes. Thus it is no accident that the outstanding examples of these high notes have been contributed by Johann Stamitz, residing at the Palatinate court at Mannheim, by Pokorny, at the Oettingen-Wallerstein and Thurn-and-Taxis courts, and by Schacht, also at the Thurn-and-Taxis court at Regensburg. These, without a doubt, were centers where the horns must have been superlative in the middle of the eighteenth century.

In the second place, the mere presence of competent players was not enough to ensure brilliant horn writing unless the composers themselves had sufficient imagination. Thanks both to the orchestras and to the composers, these brilliant eighteenth-century symphonies and concertos were written and have been preserved for us today, when (more's the pity!) their excessive demands upon the hornists will probaby not allow us to become acquainted with them save by eye and the inward ear.

ii.   The Second Horn

Although I found no part for second horn that matched the
e''' of Caldara's trumpet in Example 60, the literature contains a
fair number of instances where the horns have been directed
to play in unison as high as c'''. There was even the unison octave
leap to d''' in a Huber *Symphony in D* reported in Example 163.
The vast majority of works that include parts for high unison
horns were in D, and the unisons often came at the end of the
work, as in a Galuppi *Symphony in D* (T.&T.11) or in a similar
passage in a *Symphony in D* (DTOe XV²[31]) that was really
by G. M. Monn and not by Pokorny under an assumed name.
(Example 171) It is more difficult to leap to the unison c'''

Ex. 171

Unison Horns in D

than to approach it gradually, as Monn did; but this hazard was
presented by Pokorny (now called Abel) in an Italianate Finale
(T.&T.41), as well as by Graun (T.&T.8) in a more weighty
cadence. (Example 172)

Hasse contributed two interesting examples of high horns
playing in unison; in both, the regular succession of eighth notes

Ex. 172

Unison Horns in D

facilitated the performance. The former, Example 173, from a
D major Symphony, Op. 3/5, suggests a carillon by its descending, repeated scale. The latter, Example 174, is from an *F major
Symphony*, and is a rare instance of a second horn touching c'''
in a key as high as F. Although the horns were in counterpoint
rather than in unison, there are two works by Bach in which

Ex. 173

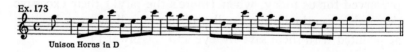

Unison Horns in D

the second horn in G reaches c'''. In *Cantata No. 128* the horns are playing florid, canonic parts above the soprano *cantus firmus*, and the second horn follows the leader as far as c''', while the first horn touches d'''. This was shown in Example 72, and a reference was made to *Cantata 174*, where the first horn also reaches d'''. In the latter work the second horn similarly goes up to c'''.

Ex. 174

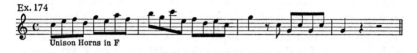

Unison Horns in F

Of course, it was an exception for horns to play in unison in their highest register. But often they played in thirds, and an octave or a tenth was the usual limit of tonal separation. Sometimes the composer conceived of the horn parts, not as a homophonic or polyphonic duet, but as a melody and bass. With no need for the tones of the two instruments to blend, wider intervals often occurred. The interval of a nineteenth was not uncommon, as from g to d''' in the Pokorny Examples 116, 117, 142 and 149, and the Stamitz Example 139; from c to g'' in the Pokorny Example 115, and an octave higher, c'-g''', in the Schacht Example 120. There was a twentieth, g-e''', in the Pokorny Example 118 and the Graun Example 147, and a triple octave, a twenty-second, in the Veichtner minuet, Example 141.

iii.   Pedal Notes

The Pokorny Example 118 contained the notes e and f, and the Graun Example 147, d, e, and f. In the Maschek Example 121 both f and f♯ appeared. None of these notes is in the harmonic series. They are so-called pedal notes, produced by a loose lip from the third harmonic, g. These were originally not stopped notes, having often been written by composers like Pokorny who made no use of the stopped-note technique.

In scores where both horn parts were written on one staff, the notation of the pedal notes was conventionally taken care of by using two clefs, the ordinary G clef on the second line for the first horn and the F clef below the first line for the second horn

—to be read, as usual, an octave higher. In the Larghetto poco Andante of the Pokorny *Double Horn Concerto in F* (T.&T. 162) there is an unusual, written-out cadenza which epitomizes even better than the Schacht Example 120 the contrasted styles of the first and second horn. Here, too, the first horn has *clarino* floridity, as well as more lyric movement. The second horn shares homophonically in the lyric parts, has a fanfare in triplet eighths and then in sixteenths, and also provides a solid bass in pedal-note quarters to the pyrotechnics of his companion. The presentation of this cadenza in Example 175 retains the original notation with two clefs for the part where the pedal notes (e, f, f♯) occur.

Ex. 175

Horns in F

Of all the pedal notes in the examples just referred to, only the d presented a problem of intonation, because it lies so far below the open g. It was present only in Example 147, from the Graun *Symphony in F*. In the first movement of this symphony, Graun has allotted the entire C major scale, from c' to c, to the second horn. (Example 176) Here also the d was the greatest hazard, since the b and a could be produced from the fourth harmonic, c'. The d also occurred in two Graun *Symphonies in D* (T.&T. 4, 6), as well as in the minuet of a Johann Stamitz *Symphony in F* (DTB F3). In the Allegro of a Sandel *Symphony in F* (T.&T.7) the second horn had to play d sixteen times in succession, with the first horn two octaves higher; at another spot in this movement there is a whole-note d. Evidently Sandel's *secondo* hornist possessed a secret of performance for this note unknown elsewhere!

Still rarer than the pedal notes for second horn just discussed (with the exception of the d) are the sub-pedal notes produced from the second harmonic, c. Example 177 is taken from a composer whose name carries weight—Joseph Haydn. The notes shown, c, B, A, G, occur identically in Nos. 2, 3, and 5 of his *Six Divertissements à 8 Parties concertantes . . .* , Op. 31, and also in his *Symphony No. 51* in B flat. The Haydn example is duplicated even to note values (the signature, however is $\frac{6}{8}$ rather

Ex. 176   Ex. 177

Horn in F   Horn in A (also in G)

than $\frac{3}{4}$) in a Romance Andantino movement of a *Symphony in C* by Wranitzky (T.&T.1), and there is an almost identical passage in the slow movement, coincidentally called Romance Andantino, of Schacht's *Double Concerto in E* (T.&T.29). Karl Stamitz, in the Andante moderato of a *Quartet in E flat* for wind and strings (T.&T.37), also has a descending progression from c to G. A somewhat different use of sub-pedal notes occurs in Emmert's *Harmonie in E flat* (T.&T.2), where, in the seventh movement, an Adagio, the horn boldly attacks the G and then slides, cadenza-like, up to the c. (Example 178)

The lowest sub-pedal note found was F♯, in the Allegro of Reicha's *Double Concerto in E*, Opus 5. The second horn plays the scale fragment c″, b′, a′, g′, f♯′, which contains three stopped notes. It then repeats this motive, either at the same pitch (note the changed notation) or else two octaves lower. (Example 179)

Ex. 178   Ex. 179

Horn in Eb   2nd Horn in E

Since there were many stopped notes in this work, especially in the Cantabile Romanza (See Example 206.), some stopping may have been used on the sub-pedal notes. (The work was published by Simrock in 1819 or '20 under the name of J. Reicha. Joseph Reicha, however, had died in 1795. The style places the concerto definitely as the work of his nephew, A. J. Reicha.) In the Allegro ma non troppo of Amon's *First Quintet in F* for wind and strings, there is a passage much like the Reicha example. Here, however, when the notes c', b, a, g, notated as usual an octave low, are to be repeated in the sub-pedal octave, they are provided with an *ossia* at the former pitch. (See Example 190.) It was not every *basso* hornist who could master these notes in the very depths!

The famous solo for fourth horn in the Adagio of Beethoven's *Ninth Symphony* contains many stopped notes. (See Example 208.) It also contains the sub-pedal G, as does the Gloria of the *Missa Solemnis* in D, where the second and fourth horns sustain it as an actual pedal. (Beethoven has used the double-clef convention to notate this passage. See *Beethoven Edition*, Vol. 18, pp. 78-80.) Beethoven has written a curious pedal chord for brass in the Scherzo of the *Ninth Symphony*. Thanks to the crooking in two different keys, the D-minor triad is sounded, with the unison D trumpets playing concert d''; the unison D horns, a'; the unison Bb *basso* horns, f'; and the timpano, f. Each brass part joins the drums on the "TIMpani" motive, with its octave leap. As the drum motive is emphatically asserted twenty times, the woodwind and strings play in octaves the subject of the fugue which began the movement. (Example 180)

Ex. 180

Woodwind and Strings

Trumpets and Horns (Concert Notation)

This same D-minor triad also occurs in the Finale of the *Ninth*. At the beginning of the Presto, it is spread out to include the concert notes F, f, d', f' on the horns, a and a' on the trumpets, and A on the timpano. (Example 181 (a)) Against this chord a clashing bb'-bb'' sounds in the upper woodwind. But when this part is repeated later, the strings are also playing (c#', e', e', g'' respectively) to complete a diminished seventh chord. Thus every note of the D-minor scale occurs simultaneously, with raucous effect. (Example 181 (b)) Ebenezer Prout (*Harmony*, p. 192f.) said that this passage was cited by Macfarren in his *Six Lectures on Harmony* as an example of the complete chord of the dominant thirteenth. Prout himself correctly states that the

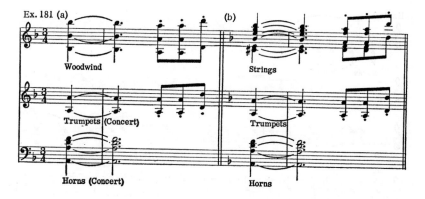

string parts constitute a quadruple appoggiatura, or, as he puts it, they are "accented auxiliary notes to the notes of the tonic chord, together with which they are sounded."

We conclude our discussion of pedal notes for horns with another example of a pedal, in the usual musical meaning of the word. In the first of Melchior's *Quatre petits duos concertants*, Op. 1, the third movement is a Louré in $\frac{6}{8}$ meter. The second horn imitates the drone of a bagpipe by sounding only g or c' as the first horn plays the melody. But Melchior evidently wanted to furnish a crude, pastoral effect, for he has only the dominant pedal in the first part, when the tonic would be more appropriate. Then the tonic pedal is used only during a modulation to A minor, and the dominant returns for a modulation to E flat major. Of all bagpipe drones, this is certainly *sui generis*. (Example 182) (Melchior's pedalpoints for second horn are more than matched by a kettledrum D which intrudes rhythmically throughout a three-phrase period in B minor in a chorus in Handel's *Joshua*. [*Handel Edition*, Vol. 17, pp. 110-112] The D is struck repeatedly against the dominant triad [F♯, A♯, C♯] or the dominant seventh.)

iv. The *Ossia*

In the Thurn and Taxis Library there are a number of works in which horn players have made emendations in their parts in pencil, ink, or even red crayon. The bulk of these changes

were made to avoid the very high notes that would never have ruffled the aplomb of the players in the heyday of the princely orchestra. For example, in the Allegro assai of a Pokorny *Symphony in E flat* (T.&T.88), the halfnote f''' is replaced by a note an octave lower, although the stratospheric eighth-note g''' is retained and also the quarter-note e'''. (Example 183) Again, in the passage from the score of a Pokorny *Symphony in E*

shown in Example 169, the first-horn part has the first e''' replaced by c''' and the f''' in the following bar by d''', although the e''' in the third bar is left unaltered. Surely the *primo* player was still a giant when these changes were made!

Fast notes were simplified in the Rondo en Chasse of Vandenbroek's *First Sinfonie Concertante in E flat* (T.&T.2). In the first excerpt shown, the ripieno horns play eighth notes where the solo horns have sixteenths—a not uncommon simplification; in a later excerpt, the first solo horn is provided with a similar *ossia*. (Examples 184 (a) and (b)) In the Andante of a Zim-

Ex. 184 (a)

Solo Horns in Eb

Ripieno Horns in Eb

(b)

Solo Horn in Eb

mermann *Symphony in B flat* (T.&T.8) a "smear" from c″ to c‴ has been changed in pencil to an arpeggio. (Example 185) In the Menuet Trio of a Fischer *Symphony in E flat* (T.&T.3), the first horn was given this same glissando, with the second horn playing an octave lower. By inking out the fast notes on the first beat, a player has emended the second-horn part to the version shown in Example 186.

Ex. 185 (a)   (b)   Ex. 186

Horn in Bb <u>basso</u>

When a short passage was emended simply by being brought down an octave, the player had evidently added stopped notes to his bag of tricks at the same time that he had ceased to cultivate the *clarino* register. There is a *Symphony in B flat* (Krul 1b/19; 1a/5) by Rosetti in which the horns are in "b hoch." When the first horn has nine bars of g″, an "8va" has been written beneath. But, right after this, the first horn is asked to play up to c‴ (almost impossible for a horn in Bb *alto*), and the four-note motive has been written an octave lower, including the stopped a′. (Example 187) In the Cantabile of Domnich's *Premier Simphonie Concertante* in F, the solo *primo* horn already has stopped notes to play; the emendation allows him to avoid any note higher than g″. (Example 188) This movement is in C minor; Domnich was one of the few composers of his age to use a key signature for horns.

Just as the highest notes were no longer playable in the

Ex. 187   Ex. 188

Horn in Bb alto   Solo Horn in F

decadent period of the Thurn and Taxis Orchestra, so were the pedal notes. The remarkable passage for two horns in E flat in the Andante Allegretto of Krommer's *Partita in B flat*, Opus 45, No. 1, must have been extremely difficult for the *secondo* player, with the abrupt changes of tessitura. As amended at Regensburg, the sub-pedal notes are raised two octaves to a simple unison with the *primo* part, with no more difficult notes to play than b′ and a′. (Example 189) The sub-pedal notes in

Ex. 189

Horns in Eb

the Amon *Quintet in F* referred to on page 143 are identical with Krommer's, but the emendation was made by raising them one octave only to their previous pitch, an indication that the notes a and b were considered easier than A and B. (Example 190)

Extensive and careful alterations have been made in a Rosetti *Horn Concerto in E flat*. To avoid the high notes, b″ and c‴, part of a passage in the Allegro molto is put down an octave; a scale passage in A minor in triplet eighths is changed to slurred

Ex. 190

Horn in F

arpeggio eighths; a trill on b" is brought down an octave, with a
different preparation; a smear in the c'-c" octave is changed to
an arpeggio, and, although c''' is still touched in the revision,
the passage ends less brilliantly in the lower octave. (Examples
191 (a), (b), (c), and (d); emendations in Examples 192 (a),
(b), (c), and (d))

Very similar, but less extensive, changes were made in the
horn parts of a Rosetti *Double Concerto in F* (or E), as played
by the Oettingen-Wallerstein Orchestra. In one of the couplets
of the *chasse* Rondo, the first horn goes scalewise to c'''; this is
tamely amended to end on e", which makes parallel octaves
with the second horn. A couple of bars later a descending fanfare for the second horn is revised; instead of g" its highest note
is c". Finally, after another two bars, a sixteenth d''' is eliminated from the first horn, although an eighth c''' is retained. Even
with the emendations, made independently in these two Rosetti
concertos, the players would have had to be real virtuosi.

Some of the emendations made at Regensburg reveal the piti-
ful state of the orchestra there shortly before its disbanding.

The note f#″ had been written for over a century for trumpet and for horn; any *secondo* player would have taken it in his stride. And yet in a Vanhal *Symphony in D* (T.&T.13), d″ was substituted in red crayon in the *primo* trumpet part for every f#″ that was written in the part—at each of these places the *primo* horn was already playing d″. In a *Parthia in E flat* (T.&T. Inc. IV(a) 16/2) by an anonymous composer, there were two horns in E flat and two in B flat. The latter were evidently in *B alto,* for the highest note was a″, although the *primo* horn in E flat went as high as c‴. Even so, there is a place where the *primo* Bb horn was asked to sustain g″ for fourteen beats, but a penciled *ossia* brings this down to c″. And in the final bars of the Alla Polacca of Krommer's *Harmonie in F,* Opus 73, a few simple flourishes that extended only to e″ in the second-horn part were evidently too difficult, for the horns exchanged their parts at this point.

Players had their difficulties with high notes in other centers also. In the third act of Caldara's opera, *I due dittatori,* there is an aria with an obbligato for trumpet in C, in which the trumpet twice makes a gradual ascent to g‴. Each passage is provided with an *ossia.* Examples 193 (a) and (b) show the

second, more elaborate passage, together with its simplified version, in which the trumpet still must finish with a half-note c‴. In the fifth act of this opera the second trumpet imitates the first in a similar ornamented scale that reaches e‴, as was shown in Example 160.

Far removed from the tonal level of Caldara's trumpets are the trumpet parts of Vivaldi's *Gloria*, which needed no *ossias* because of high notes. Here the emender has been the modern editor, Alfredo Cassella, who has gratuitously given the first trumpet an f' and the second trumpet d', f', and b—all impossible in Vivaldi's time. (Example 194 (a)) A few pages later he has added lower octaves in a trumpet passage which does not rise above the written e''; here d' appears again. In the Cum Sancto Spiritu, although he has allowed the first trumpet to play a half-note a'' in a polyphonic passage, he has dropped the first trumpet an octave in one motive, apparently to avoid g''. Three pages later he has similarly dropped the second trumpet an octave, thereby encountering the forbidden notes, a', f', and f#'. (Example 194 (b))

Ex. 194 (a)   (b)

Trumpets in D   Trumpet in D
(Concert Notation)

But the editorial changes made in the Vivaldi trumpet parts are mild compared to some of the editing done by Robert Sondheimer. In a *Symphony in G* by J. C. Bach, dated 1760, the stopped notes, d', f', and a', were written for the horns, although Hampel did not discover stopping until after this date. The date of the Rigel *Symphony in C minor*, Opus 12, No. 4, is 1769. In the Sondheimer edition the scoring is for two oboes, three horns in E flat, and strings. The horns are asked to play such stopped notes as d', f', f#', g#', a', b', c#'', d#'' (eb''), and g#''. The sophisticated style of the horn parts here is wholly at variance with the brevity and simplicity of the work.

Sondheimer's lack of taste is the most irritating feature of his additions to eighteenth-century works. In the Andante of Christian Cannabich's *G major Symphony* of 1760, for flutes, horns, and strings, Sondheimer has added an elaborate part for modern piano, which sticks out like a picture window on a sharecropper's cabin. His worst offense is in a Polaci *D major Symphony*, dated about 1745. The original symphony was in three movements: Maestoso, Andante, and Menuett; it appears to have been an Italian overture. To this, Sondheimer has tacked on a Grave in D minor (!), the first movement of a French overture, which had no connection originally with the other three movements. For the added movement he has written extremely rich and complex parts for four horns, Wagnerian in character, and bristling with notes unplayable on the natural horn. The way of the transgressor *should* be hard!

Chapter V

Conclusion

❧

i. Stopped Notes

The main purpose of this book has been to show what composers were able to accomplish with trumpets and horns within the very narrow bounds of the harmonic series. The use of notes foreign to the series might then have been regarded as not quite cricket, like cheating at solitaire. But, paradoxically, at the very time that the horn assumed the distinctive timbre with which we now associate it, it also was given the possibility of a greatly expanded scale. So, many of our illustrations have included stopped notes. In the previous chapter we had also been considering "factitious" notes at the lower end of the compass.

But stopped notes and pedal notes were not the only type of factitious note employed by composers on occasion. As a lower neighbor to c″, the note b′ was considered wholly legitimate. Written for trumpet, the b′ occurred in Examples 27 and 32, and, as the only extra-series note for horn, in Examples 46, 55, 63, 108, 111, 134, and 184. Of course, the eleventh harmonic often served as f♯″, although more commonly as f″.

Because f♯″ and both b♭′ and b♭″ were reasonably close to pitches of the harmonic series, it was easy enough for the trumpet as well as the horn to play in G minor, provided that the Dorian form of the scale was used. In Johann Kaspar Fischer's *Journal du Printemps* for two trumpets and five-part strings, there is a passage in thirds for trumpets, with a cadence in G minor. (Example 195 (a)) In the Entrée of the same work, in a modulation to A minor, the neighboring b' appears, as well as the very rare g#''. (Example 195 (b)) The thirteenth harmonic was used regularly for a'', but is even flatter than the eleventh harmonic is sharp for f''. (When f'' and a'' were sounded together in the subdominant triad, considerable adjustment was necessary in order to make the third acceptable. Note that unforced harmonics 8 and 10 form the pure major third, 9 and 11 a flattened

Ex. 195 (a)

Trumpets in C

(b)

major third, 10 and 12 a pure minor third, and 11 and 13 a flattened *minor* third!)

Since the thirteenth harmonic came so close to g#'', the note could be used safely. The wonder is that it was not employed more frequently than it was. Fischer, in the passage shown, first treats the g#'' conservatively as a lower neighbor; he then boldly asserts it, but as forming the dissonant tritone with d''; in the cadence its imprecise intonation is disguised by a trill. Sebastian Bach mercilessly exposed the g#'' in the trumpet's *cantus firmus* of "Ein' feste Burg," referred to on page 75. In the famous horn obbligato in the Quoniam of the *B minor Mass* there is a trilled g#'', and in *Hercules* (Example 52) the first horn plays a sixteenth-note g#''.

In Handel's *Concerto for Two Choirs* the first horn plays an eighth-note g#'', approached by skip from e', and in his opera, *Arianna*, there is a g#'', which is both approached and quitted by skip. Pokorny's use of the g#'', as in Examples 54, 58, and 59, is another illustration of a factitious note obtained without hand-stopping.

A note that requires more adjustment than g#'' is c#''. Like the ubiquitous b', it could be used as a lower neighbor to d'', as in a trumpet duet in Bach's *Cantata 31* (Example 50), where its uncertain intonation in the cadence may have been disguised by a trill. It was also used as a neighbor in a chorus in this cantata, in which there is a canonic duet between the trumpet and first violins. In *Cantata 41*, "Jesu, nun sei gepreiset," when the first trumpet in C plays the chorale melody as a *cantus firmus* with the sopranos, one phrase ends in D minor, and here the half-note c♯'' must have been more difficult to control. (Example 196)

Ex. 196

Trumpet in C

In the Agnus Dei of Kerll's *Missa à tre cori* in C, there is a motive in D major in which the second trumpet plays c♯'' as a neighbor, and then this is sequentially repeated in E minor, with d♯'' similarly treated. (Example 197) The d♯'' is, of course, analogous to other notes a semitone below a note in the harmonic series. Bach has written the synonymous note, e♭'', in *Der zufriedengestellte Aeolus*, in a passage where the three trumpets

Ex. 197

Trumpets in C

play accompanying chords. Since the chord in question is a diminished triad, c'' e♭'' a'', any imprecision in the intonation of the factitious note would have been excusable.

In the light of the eighteenth-century employment of the factitious notes for trumpet, let us examine some odd notes in Fantini's collection of 1638. In his capriccio, *Carducci*, the notes a', f', and d' occur as upper neighbors, and were probably played by forcing the sixth, fifth, and fourth harmonics respectively. (Example 198 (a)) (In another of the little pieces a neighboring a' occurs nine times.) In the call, *l'Accavallo*,

Ex. 198 (a)

Trumpet in C or D

there is a sixteenth-note d' in the succession c', d', e'. Here the intent seems to have been a smear, as in some of the octave scales of the eighteenth century. (Example 198 (b)) In one of his exercises there is a tremolando g#". (Example 198 (c)) In his eleventh ricercata, *l'Albergotti*, the c#" occurs in a cadence in D minor. (Example 198 (d)) Also, in his first sonata for trumpet and organ, *Colloretto*, a dotted-quarter c#" occurs. This note has prompted Menke to conclude that the pieces were played on the *Jägertrommel*, which, because it was coiled, offered a chance for hand-stopping. (Menke, *History*, p. 53) But there is no reason to believe that this c#", as well as the other notes shown, could not have been controlled by the player's lips as well in the 17th century as in the 18th century. (Maurice Peress in an article in *Brass Quarterly* for Spring, 1961 refers to certain puzzling notes in Fantini, which he says can be played on a late 17th-century Haas trumpet in his possession. He mentions a', b', and eb" as easily obtained, d' and f' as more difficult but suitable for passing notes.) Taking Fantini's out-of-series notes as a whole, one must consider them a fascinating anticipation of certain procedures that were rare, but not absent, in trumpet and horn music a century later than his time.

Usually, when notes foreign to the harmonic series were played on brass instruments in the latter part of the eighteenth century, it was as stopped notes on horns. The origin of the stopping principle is inseparably connected with the modern position of the horn, with the hand in the bell. This position was first used in the seventh decade of the eighteenth century by Anton Joseph Hampel, who discovered that it improved the tone of the horn greatly, taking away all the hoarseness and harshness of the *cor de chasse* and substituting a softer, rounder tone more suitable for symphonic use. But the presence of the hand in the bell, as the horn was normally held, lowered the pitch by a semitone.

As Hampel experimented with deeper hand positions, he found that an insertion two or three times as great (quarter or half stopping) would lower the pitch by another semitone, and four times as great (three-quarter stopping) by a tone. But when the horn was completely stopped, that is, five times as much as normal, the pitch was the same as when the hand was not inserted at all—thus raising the normal pitch a semitone (Paul, *Das Horn*, pp. 79-84).

Thus, with the aid of stopping, it would be possible to play any note above c′, since, for example, c♯′ was obtained from c′ by whole stopping, and d′ and e♭′ from the open e′ by three-quarter and one-quarter stopping respectively. Stopping gave a somewhat dry and muted quality to the tone, and both composers and players had to consider this fact and to favor the stopped tones. According to Paul, the contrast between open and stopped tones was greater in Germany than in France and Italy, and so Berlioz, for example, freely wrote stopped notes that came off less satisfactorily in German performance.

Although the stopped note offered great possibilities for chromatic alterations and distant modulations, it was even more valuable for completing the diatonic scale in the lower octave. Since the seventh harmonic produced a very flat b♭′, little stopping was required for a satisfactory a′. Examples 104 and 119 contain G-major scales by Rosetti and Beethoven respectively in which no rarer pitches occur than b′ and a′, and these notes also appear in the Rosetti *ossias* of Examples 187 and 192. In Mozart's Larghetto, with the horn playing in the written key of F, the a′ is shown in Example 131. The f♯′ was another note which could be produced easily by stopping. Occurring as a neighboring note in Example 170, it probably was produced just by the lips. But, in Example 179, as the final note in a sequence which also included b′ and a′, it must have been stopped.

The notes d′ and f′ were more difficult to produce, since they required three-quarter stopping. These were two of the Rosetti stopped notes in Example 191 which were omitted in the emended version, Example 192. In the Allegro moderato of the Domnich *Sinfonia concertante in F* from which Example 188 had been taken, the active second horn plays f′ and d′ as eighth notes, leaping upward a tenth from the latter. Observe that most of these notes were staccato, so that a glissando was not to be considered. (Example 199) In the Rondo of Punto's *Seventh Concerto* in F, there is a descending scale in eighths to d′, with the same upward leap to f″.

There is a puzzling use of d′, f′, and a′ for trumpets in **D** in
the final chorus of Buxtehude's cantata, "Ihr lieben Christen."
(Example 200) In the first bar both trumpets leap to the d′, and
in the third bar, although all the factitious notes are in a stepwise
progression, they are at times accented. Since Buxtehude has

Ex. 199

Horns in F

written only notes in the harmonic series for his trumpets elsewhere in this cantata, this one appearance of impossible notes
is startling. Perhaps they were intended to be played an octave
higher, which would have offered no difficulties.

The key of G became easier for horns with a bit of stopping.
The scales by Rosetti and Beethoven (Examples 104 and 119)

Ex. 200

Trumpets in D

have already been mentioned. Example 48, also from the
Beethoven *Sextet,* is in G, and includes the chromatic neighbors, d♯″ and c♯″. There is a modulation to G in the Gallay
Example 132, with stopped notes, d′, f♯′, a′, and b′. Also,
Weber's F horns must play in G in Example 133, and they play
the stopped scale notes, d′, f♯′, a′ and b′, as well as the chromatic
passing note, d♯″.

Despite the relative ease of the stopping required, the key of
F seems to have been one of the least promising keys for modulations which included horns. In Example 133, Weber's C horns
modulate to F by way of the open note, b♭′, as Mozart's horn
does to assert this key in Example 131. Beethoven's chamber
music for wind and strings also contains good examples of horns
playing in F major: in the Adagio of the *Sextet,* from which
two of our examples have been drawn, and in the Allegro con
brio of the *Septet,* Opus 20.

We have already noted, in Examples 50, 196, and 198 (d),
that composers sometimes wrote c♯″ for trumpet, as the leading

note of D minor. With the c#″ stopped, modulations to D minor were easy for horns. (Examples 105 and 107 show c#″ as a chromatic passing note.) Although it was possible to play in G minor in the upper octave without using any stopped notes, as Fischer's trumpet did in Example 195, the harmonic form of the scale was more common, and this would include at least the stopped eb″. In the Allegro maestoso of his *Second Horn Concerto* in E flat, Mozart did use the harmonic form of G minor, with a striking upward leap of a diminished seventh, f#′-eb″, which involves both of the essential notes of this mode. The second phrase is a variant of the first, with slightly varied stress upon the two important stopped notes. (Example 201) The Dauprat Example 127 (b) also has a leap from f#′ to eb″.

Ex. 201

Horn in Eb

To judge from the abundance of examples, the key of A minor seems to have been popular with eighteenth-century writers for brass. However, in Examples 52, 54, 58, and 59 the leading note of this key appeared as g#″, a note which did not absolutely require stopping. In Example 191 (b) there was an A-minor scale in triplets from c‴ to f#′. The *ossia* in Example 192 (b) eliminated both g#″ and g#′, but the latter would have been the more difficult note. In the Allegro of Mozart's *Third Horn Concerto* in E flat there is a short passage in which three g#′ emphasize the A-minor tonality. The first being a lower neighbor to a′, its intonation is not so important as in the following bar, where the note is needed to outline the triad of E major. (Example 202)

Neither D nor B flat is a key to which modulations are often made. In the Haydn Adagio in Example 123, D was the dominant of the dominant; the c#‴ is, of course, not a stopped note. The key of B flat was not quite so rare. The most interesting modulation to that key occurred in the Romance Allegretto of

Krommer's *Partita in E flat*, Opus 45, No. 2. Krommer has given the first horn a warm, lyric melody in binary form, forty bars in length with the repetitions. Beginning in G, it comes to a cadence in B flat at the end of the first strain; at the end of the second strain it returns to G. The thrice-occurring appog-

Ex. 202

Horn in Eb

giatura c#″ is a feature of this melody, in which eb″ is the only other stopped note. (Example 203)

We have seen that compositions or movements in minor keys were often scored for brass in the tonic key, despite the comparatively few open notes that were then available. With the advent of hand-stopping, the horns were much better equipped to play in C minor. In the rondo Finales of Rosetti's horn concertos, there would regularly be couplets in C minor and A

Ex. 203

Horn in Eb

minor. In other movements, too, Rosetti would use horns in modulations to C minor, as in Example 135, from the Romance Adagio non tanto of a *Double Concerto in F* (or E). This lovely melody contains a further modulation to E flat.

Example 127 (a), from Dauprat's *Third Horn Concerto* in E, is also in C minor, and resembles the Rosetti melody in the turn near the beginning. Both of these illustrations contain the stopped notes, f′, ab′, eb″, and ab″, and the former has, in addition, eb′ for second horn. Observe also that the chromatic passage from Domnich's Cantabile in Example 188 is in C minor, and that Melchior's Louré in Example 182 modulates both to C minor and to E flat.

Beethoven rejoiced in opportunities for his horns to play in C minor. On page 104 reference was made to the *tutti* near the beginning of the *Ninth Symphony*, in which the D horns play the stopped notes, eb' and eb''. In the first movement of the *Eroica Symphony* in E flat the first and second horns present a minor version of the principal, fanfaring motive. Also, in the Introduction to the oratorio, *The Mount of Olives*, the horns in E flat outline the C minor triad, c', eb', g', c''. The curious reader will have no difficulty in locating these three illustrations of C minor for horns in the works of Beethoven.

Like the latter two Beethoven illustrations, Schubert's *Eine kleine Trauermusik* for nine wind instruments is in the concert key of E flat minor; so that the Eb horns play in C minor, with stopped notes throughout. The first section, which the horns play alone, modulates to E flat; in the second section the first strain recurs and continues to a cadence in C minor. Tempting as it would be to present Schubert's horns in the *Trauermusik*, we shall pass this up in favor of a striking passage in this same concert key of E flat minor, found in the Introduction Adagio of Dauprat's *Third Quintet for Horn and Strings*. The composer himself says of this: "Ou l'on voit l'étendue que peut parcourir le second Cor sur le ton de Mi bemol." Here the total compass is three and a half octaves, G-c''' (it is intended for a *cor-basse*), and the stopped notes include f, ab, eb', ab', eb'', and ab'', with some stopping probably needed for the sub-pedal Bb, Ab, and G. (Example 204)

Ex. 204

Horn in Eb

Schacht has provided a dramatic effect at the very end of the Adagio movement of a *C major Symphony* (T.&T.21). This movement is in F minor. The horns, having remained in C, now play in unison for the concluding bars. The stopped db'' is blared forth each time it occurs, and at the end is resolved on a pianissimo c''. (Example 205) Participation in this Phrygian cadence is the only chance the horns have to display their particular talents in this entire symphony. (In a *Quartet in C for*

Horn and Strings (T.&T.54), Schacht has an imaginative use of c♯'' and e♭'' as appoggiaturas to d''.) For really lyric melody in F minor, see the Cantabile Romanza of Reicha's *Concerto Concertant in E for Horns and Orchestra* (T.&T.3). The movement is in A minor, and, as in the Schacht Adagio just referred to, the horns do not change their crook, and so play in F minor

Ex. 205

Unison Horns in C

throughout. The excerpt shown in Example 206 has imitative writing for the horns, and includes the stopped notes, f', a♭', d♭'', e♭'', and a♭''.

Another rare glimpse of F minor occurs in Haydn's *Trumpet Concerto in E flat*. Although written for a keyed trumpet, most of this composition could be played on a stopped horn, as indicated by Example 106. The Andante would have presented

Ex. 206

Horns in E

problems, but not unsurmountable ones. The passage shown in Example 207 begins in F minor and modulates to A flat. It includes the stopped notes, d♭', d', e♭', f', a♭', d♭'', and e♭''.

Except for such incidental cadencing as just shown, the key of A flat lies beyond the scope of the stopped horn. It was not that the individual notes in the key were unplayable; it was probably rather that the remoteness of the tonal center from

Ex. 207

Keyed Trumpet in E♭

fixed points of reference in the harmonic series made it seem an *ultima Thule*. Thus the famous solo for fourth horn in E flat in the Adagio of Beethoven's *Ninth Symphony* appears all the more remarkable. (Example 208) It begins with the four-note opening motive of the movement, e'', b', c'', g', repeats the motive varied an octave lower, and then enters the sub-pedal

octave with a final repetition of the descending fourth, c-G.
After this cadenza-like beginning, there is a change to a normal
tessitura and the key of A flat, in which the appoggiatura db'',
c'' occurs three times, although not so blatantly as in the
Schacht Example 205. Just after the part given, Beethoven has
written an octave scale in A flat for the horn.

Ex. 208

It has been stated, upon insufficient evidence, that Beethoven's
solo for fourth horn had been written to be played on a valved
horn by Eduard C. Lewy, who had come to Vienna in 1822.
W. F. H. Blandford (see his article, "The Fourth Horn in the
'Choral Symphony,'") is convinced that Beethoven did not
write the part for a valved horn, although Lewy may well have
played in the first performance. The passage could have been
played well enough on a stopped horn. In the light of
Beethoven's calculated treatment of stopped notes elsewhere, I
believe that he intended to exploit here also the nuances of
timbre inherent in the stopping technique.

If A flat major was *terra incognita* for the valveless horn,
what shall we say about B flat minor? The only example found
was in the second strain of the first minuet of Krommer's *Concertino in D*, Opus 80. (This work is a nonet for wind and
strings. It is an arrangement by Krommer of his string quintet
of the same opus number.) This minuet is in D minor, that is,
the written key of C minor for the horns. And so the passage
in B flat minor is not really remote in its context. The second
horn is silent here, and the first horn plays in a very soft and
sustained manner in the unusual key. (Example 209) It will be
observed that the stopped notes present (a', db'', eb'') have all
occurred in previous examples.

It is understandable that stopped horns should have played
extensively in certain flat keys, not only because of the com-

mon practice of providing a movement in a minor key with
horns in the parallel major, but also because a movement in a
major key often had an extended section in the parallel minor,
as in the couplets of Rosetti's rondo Finales. So C minor and
keys closely related to it were familiar to players on the stopped
horn.

Ex. 209

Modulations to keys on the sharp side of the horn's tonal
center were rarer in the latter part of the eighteenth century, as
Table 4 reveals. Of course, G major would always be present,
and we have seen illustrations of stopped notes in that key, as
well as a cadence in D major. (Example 123) Kerll, in Example
197, modulated to E minor with trumpets. Only two horn
cadences in E minor were found, Example 210 showing such a
cadence from Cherubini's opera, *Anacréon*, as given by Coar.
Bach has a similar cadence in the "concerto" (the re-orchestrated
first movement of the *Third Brandenburg Concerto*) of his *Cantata 174*.

Ex. 210

The key of A major is neatly represented by a phrase in the
coda of the Finale of Mozart's *Serenade No. 12* in C minor,
K 388. The horns, being in E flat for the entire composition,
play in the written key of A when the concert key changes to
C major in the coda. (Example 211) As for F sharp minor, it
too was found, in Méhul's *Melidore et Prosine,*—another con-

Ex. 211

tribution by Coar. (Example 212) Note, however, that the stopped notes (f#' and c#") in the given passage belong diatonically to a key that is no more remote than D major.

The most remote sharp key was encountered in one of Duvernoy's *Douze petits Duos pour deux cors*. No. 11, a Larghetto, is in the written key of B minor, with a Trio in B

Ex. 212

Horns in Eb

major, the latter being given complete in Example 213. The five-sharp signature is true to the original. Although the stopped notes (f#', c#", d#") in this Trio are no more difficult than those in many of our other examples, and the intervals are easy, the intonation may have been hazardous. The only open note in this passage, e", is a poor anchor for the many stopped notes.

Ex. 213

Horns (in Eb?)

In several of the illustrations already shown, composers had taken advantage of their expanded resources through the stopping technique and had written chromatic progressions. This was a virtual impossibility on the natural horn except in such successions as g", f#", f", e", or c", b', bb', a' or, in the sub-pedal range, c, B, Bb, A, Ab, G. Thus, in Example 188, Domnich extended one of the pre-Hampel chromatic successions from c" down to g'; but, interestingly enough, this was presented as the *ossia* for a succession an octave higher, which needed little or no stopping.

In the Andante of Haydn's *Trumpet Concerto* (Example 207) the six-note chromatic succession, c' up to f', could have been played by a stopped horn. Mozart, whose *Second Horn Concerto* (Example 201) contains a five-note succession, bb'-d", has a six-note succession, e"-b, in the Allegro of his *C minor Serenade*. (Example 211, showing horns playing in the written key of A major, was taken from the Finale of this work.) Then, in the Rondo of his *Piano Quintet in E flat,* K 452, he extended this to an eight-note succession, e″-a′.

Beethoven has matched Mozart's eight-note succession by a rising chromatic progression from g′ to d″ in the aria, "Komm, Hoffnung," in *Fidelio.* Even with the Adagio tempo, these six bars for the three horns are strikingly different from the horn parts in the remainder of the opera. (Example 214)

Ex. 214

In the excerpt from Beethoven's *Sextet* in Example 48, there were chromatic lower neighbors and passing notes. In the more romantic type of melody of the Beethoven era the chromatic appoggiatura was a favorite coloristic device, such as Domnich's d♯″ in Example 199. This was exploited to the full by Krommer in the G major-B flat major melody of Example 203, with the recurring appoggiatura c♯″, and as anticipated dramatically by Schacht in Example 205, with its d♭″.

Sometimes the characteristic timbre of the stopped note was intensified by a *sforzando,* as in the *Horn Trio* of the *Eroica Symphony,* where the a♭ in the third horn is the key to the effect of the passage. (Example 215) In the recapitulation of the first movement of this symphony, the first horn, momentarily in F, plays a sustained g″ with a crescendo, followed by a soft a♭″— the stopped quality giving added color to the *piano* note. Similarly, in the *Overture to Coriolanus,* Beethoven has had his second horn play d″, e♭″ four times, each time with a *sforzando* on the d″. Mozart, in the Allegro maestoso of his *Serenade*

No. 11 in E flat, K 375, obtains an effect even stronger than Beethoven's in Example 215. Here he has his horns play in unison a *forte* g#′, which then tapers off to a *pianissimo*. (Example 216)

In Example 125 Krommer had combined his horns in E flat and in B flat *basso* to obtain some rich chromatic harmony,

Ex. 215

Horns in Eb

making use of the stopped notes c#″ (db″) and d#″ (eb″). In Example 203 he had written a warm, lyric melody for solo horn, using the same stopped notes. As a final illustration of Krommer's charming style for horns, there is a passage in the Adagio of his *Harmonie in C*, Opus 76, where the horns in F play most expressively, with a minimum of stopped notes, g#′ and c#″ for the second horn and eb″ for the first horn. (Example 217) Note

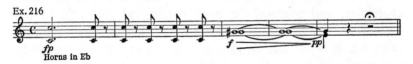

Ex. 216

Horns in Eb

the little flourish for second horn on the second ending, an amusing remnant of the practice of an earlier generation. Here Krommer has shown himself the master of the stopped technique and not its slave.

Thus in many ways the stopped horn made its presence felt toward the end of the eighteenth century and in the early decades of the nineteenth: in chromatic appoggiaturas that

Ex. 217

Horns in F

were a legitimate extension of the horn's expressive powers; in chromatic progressions that belied the very nature of the horn as brass instrument; in modulations to distant keys like B major and B-flat minor, where the intonation must have been as uncertain as the steering of a ship without a compass on a starless night. The advent of valved trumpets and horns must have brought to many a player a feeling of relief.

ii.   Prospect and Retrospect

During the course of the nineteenth century the horn began to be prized most highly for qualities that were only dimly perceived a few decades earlier. The just-shown Adagio by Krommer (Example 217) was a harbinger of the new fashion; the prayer-like Adagio of the *Freischütz Overture* (Example 133) was in the mode; Mendelssohn's Nocturne (Example 134) was of its very essence. At the end of the century Ebenezer Prout could sincerely say: "The tone of the horn is one of the most expressive, and perhaps the most poetic and romantic in the orchestra. Though sometimes used for lively solos, hunting calls, &c, it is far better adapted for dreamy and melancholy passages." [Ebenezer Prout, *The Orchestra*, Vol. 1, p. 184]

It is nonsense to say that the horn is "better adapted" to play expressive melody than to play the brilliant passages assigned to it by eighteenth-century composers like Bach and Pokorny. But certainly the horn, especially the stopped and valved horn, is well equipped to play "dreamy and melancholy passages." The Romantic composers were fond of exploiting this emasculated part of horn technique. Its ruder, more virile functions as a solo instrument were largely relinquished to the trumpet. The Andante Cantabile of Tchaikovsky's *Fifth Symphony* typically reveals the horn of the later Romanticists on its very best behavior. But Brahms followed the elegiac slow movement of his *Horn Trio* by a breathless Finale in which one can almost see the baying hounds. And surely Punto, most famous of *cor-basse* players, would have relished the swooping arpeggios by which Strauss depicted his rapscallion, Till.

With the exception of examples of hand-stopping, this book

has been only slightly concerned with the horn as an instrument for emotional expression. Up to the end of the eighteenth century the horn was treated like a more versatile type of trumpet, adept enough at fanfares and fiorituras, jealously conserving the *sonneries de la chasse*, rising to dizzy tonal heights in an Allegro or a minuet Trio.

As we have seen, the great Baroque composers, Bach and Handel, wrote brilliantly for both trumpets and horns. Both men were masters of the florid *clarino* style; both were at times indifferent to clashes caused by low-pitched arpeggios; both had a knack for combining a brass instrument with another instrument or a voice; both used the brass to double polyphonic voice parts. But, for every nuance of brass treatment in Bach and Handel, there was ample precedent from the past, whether from Schütz and Praetorius (Examples 75 and 76), Steffani and Caldara (Examples 20, 31, 32, 77; 39, 160, 193), or Buxtehude and Biber (Examples 36 and 37).

Of the great Classic composers, Joseph Haydn was, on the whole, a mediocre writer for brass. His trumpets were downright dull—in Example 95 he even tried to make them sound like horns. Haydn's horns were respectable enough. But only exceptionally did they glow, as in the exciting hunt of *The Seasons* (Example 156), the floridity of the *First Horn Concerto* (Examples 123 and 162), the soaring thirds of the *Sinfonie Concertante* (Example 47).

The Mozart illustrations include such diverse items as undiluted fanfares (Examples 17 and 103) and floridity (Example 105), expressive melodies laced with stopped notes (Examples 131 and 201), a *chasse Finale* (Example 154). Understanding the horn, Beethoven made excellent use of its stopped notes for color and as chromatic neighbors and passing notes. (Examples 48, 119, 214, 215) Wholly admirable is his exaltation of the banal "horn progression" of Gluck and a hundred second-raters, the better to strike an authentic note of cosmic joy. (Example 86)

Just as the late Baroque composers were continuing a substantial *clarino* tradition rooted in the seventeenth century, just so did the Viennese Classicists have their Bavarian precursors. But this time it was the earlier generation of composers that showed themselves supremely great, as they carefully constructed their melodies from the extended range made available through the skill of their colleagues, the horn players. It is no mere coincidence that Stamitz once pushed a horn to concert c''' (Example 139), and that both Schacht and Pokorny attained b''. (Examples 120 and 142)

But, over and over again, even when the extreme notes did not occur, there was a tremendous sweep to Stamitz' horn parts, often in octaves or larger intervals, a sweep that is unexcelled by any other composer. With Pokorny a more *cantabile* style was in evidence, and he excelled at contrasting his two horns, with widely ranging parts. Schacht was versatile enough to manipulate two pairs of horns, to insert stopped notes with calm assurance, and to outdo the old *clarino* composers in their own bailiwick. Thus, for one brief moment, in Bavaria, the horn was a proudly vaulting Pegasus; thereafter, its wings safely clipped, it was groomed for a safer rôle—the instrument of poetry and romance.

Index of Musical Examples
Arranged by Composer or Editor

Where known, the instrumental works are identified numerically. If listed or printed in one of the *Denkmäler* series, German (DDT), Bavarian (DTB), or Austrian (DTOe), this is indicated. For works consulted at the Thurn and Taxis Library (T. & T.), there is a complete reference; a symphony by Hasse was seen at the Gesellschaft der Musikfreunde (GdMF), a concerto by W. F. Bach at the Austrian National Library (NB), and two concertos by Rosetti at Oettingen-Wallerstein (Oet-Wal).

Bibliography

Since this book is based almost completely upon the original musical sources, there is no need to pad the present bibliography with numerous references to books on instruments, opera, oratorio, and symphony, as well as on the major composers included in the study. This is a working bibliography, including only those books and articles that have been of service or that are referred to in the text.

Abraham, Gerald. See Menke.

Altenburg, Johann Ernst, *Versuch einer Anleitung zur heroisch-musikalischen Trompeter- und Pauker-Kunst*, Halle, J. C. Hendel, 1795.

Apel, Willi, *Harvard Dictionary of Music*, Cambridge, Harvard University Press [1944].

Barbour, J. Murray, "Franz Krommer and His Writing for Brass," *Brass Quarterly*, Vol. 1, No. 1, Sept., 1957.

Barbour, J. Murray, "Pokorny Vindicated," *Musical Quarterly*, Vol. XLIX, No. 1, January, 1963.

Barbour, J. Murray, "Unusual Brass Notation in the Eighteenth Century," *Brass Quarterly*, Vol. 3, No. 3, June, 1959.

Birkhoff, George D., *Aesthetic Measure*, Cambridge, Harvard University Press, 1933.

Blandford, W. F. H., "The Fourth Horn in the 'Choral Symphony,'" *Musical Times*, Vol. 66, 1925, pp. 29-32.

Blandford, W. F. H., "The French Horn in England," *Musical Times*, Vol. 63, 1922, pp. 544-547.

Blandford, W. F. H., "Handel's Horn and Trombone Parts," *Musical Times*, Vol. 80, 1939, pp. 697 ff., 746 f., 794.

Blandford, W. F. H., "Wagner and the Horn Parts of *Lohengrin*," *Musical Times*, Vol. 63, 1922, pp. 622 ff., 693-697.

Boursier de la Roche, Charles, *Les plus belles fanfares de chasse*, Paris, Librairie Cynégétique, 1930.

Carse, Adam von Ahn, *Musical Wind Instruments*, London, Macmillan, 1939.

Carse, Adam von Ahn, *The Orchestra in the 18th Century*, Cambridge, W. Heffer & Sons, 1940.

de Champgrand. See Goury.

Chapman, Roger E. See Mersenne.

The Coach-Horn: What to Blow and How to Blow it, by An Old Guard, 6th ed., London, Köhler, 19 - -.

Coar, Birchard, *A Critical Study of the 19th Century Horn Virtuosi in France*, De Kalb, Ill., The Author, 1952.

Coar, Birchard, *The French Horn*, Ann Arbor, The Author, 1947.

Duvernoy, Frédéric, *Méthode pour le Cor* . . . , Op. 15, Nouvelle ed. Offenback S/M, J. André, ca. 1880.

Einstein, Alfred, *Beispielsammlung zur Musikgeschichte*, 4. Auflage, Leipzig & Berlin, Teubner, 1930.

Färber, Sigfrid, "Das Regensburger Fürstlich Thurn & Taxissche Hoftheater und seine Oper, 1760-1786," *Verhandlungen des Historischen Vereins von Oberpfalz und Regensburg*, 86. Band, 1936.

Fantini, Girolamo, *Modo per imparare a sonare di tromba*, Francofort, D. Vuastch, 1638; facsimile ed., Milano, Bolletino Bibliografico Musicale, 1934.

Goury de Champgrand, Charles Jean, *Almanach du chasseur ou calendrier perpétuel*, Paris, Pissot, 1773.

Kappey, J. A., *Military Music*, Boosey & Co., London & New York [1894].

Kastner, Georges, *Manuel général de musique militaire*, Paris, Didot Frères, 1848.

Klug, H., "Le cor de chasse," *Revista musicale italiana*, vol. 18, 1911, pp. 95-136.

Landon, H. C. Robbins, *The Symphonies of Joseph Haydn*, London, Universal Ed. & Rockliff, 1955.

Nouveau Larousse Illustré, Paris, Librairie Larousse, [1898-1904].

LaRue, Jan, "A New Figure in the Haydn Masquerade," *Music & Letters*, Vol. 40, No. 2, April, 1959.

LaRue, Jan, "Major and Minor Mysteries of Identification in the 18th-Century Symphony," *Journal of American Musicological Society*, Vol. XIII, Nos. 1-3, 1960.

Menke, Werner, *History of the Trumpet of Bach and Handel*, Eng. trans., Gerald Abraham, London, Wm. Reeves, 1934.

Mersenne, Marin, *Harmonie Universelle*, Paris, S. Cramoisy, 1636/37; *The Books on Instruments*, trans., Roger E. Chapman, The Hague, Martinus Nijhoff, 1957.

Mettenleiter, Dominicus, *Musikgeschichte der Stadt Regensburg*, Regensburg,   ,   .

Mooser, R. Aloys, *Annales de la musique et des musiciens en Russie au xviii siècle*. Tome III. Geneva, Editions du Mont-Blanc, 1951.

Nef, Karl, *Geschichte der Sinfonie und Suite*, Leipzig, Breitkopf & Härtel, 1921.

An Old Guard. See *The Coach-Horn.*

Paul, Ernst, *Das Horn in seiner Entwicklung vom Natur- zum Ventilinstrument*, Vienna Dissertation, 1932.

Peress, Maurice, "A Baroque Trumpet Discovered in Greenwich Village," *Brass Quarterly*, Vol. 4, No. 3, Spring, 1961.

Piersig, Fritz, *Die Einführung des Hornes in die Kunstmusik und seine Verwendung bis zum Tode Johann Sebastian Bachs*, Halle, M. Niemeyer, 1927.

Prout, Ebenezer, *Harmony, Its Theory and Practice*, 13th ed., London, Augener Ltd., 1903.

Prout, Ebenezer, *The Orchestra.* Vol. 1, 3rd ed., London, Augener [1897].

Ringer, Alexander Lothar, *The Chasse: Historical and Analytical Bibliography of a Musical Genre*, Columbia Dissertation, 1955.

de la Roche. See Boursier.

Schering, Arnold, *Geschichte der Musik in Beispielen*, Leipzig, Breitkopf & Härtel, 1931.

Schünemann, Georg. See *Trompeterfanfaren* . . . .

Speets, D., *De Trompet*, Hilversum, Musica Bibliotheck J. J. Lispet, 195-.

Terry, Charles Sanford, *Bach's Orchestra*, London, Oxford University Press, H. Milford, 1932.

Trompeterfanfaren, Sonaten und Feldstücke, ed., Georg Schünemann, *Das Erbe deutscher Musik*, Band 7, Kassel, Bärenreiter, 1936.

Walter, Horst, *Franz Krommer (1759-1831). Sein Leben und Werk, mit besonderer Berücksichtung des Streichquartetts*, Vienna Dissertation, 1932.

General Index